STUDY SMART

KAREN TUI BOYES

SPECTRUM EDUCATION LIMITED

Published by Spectrum Education Limited,

P O Box 30 818, Lower Hutt, New Zealand
ISBN 978-0-9876647-4-7

Text copyright © Karen Boyes 2004 revised 2018

Designed and typeset by Spectrum Education, New Zealand
Illustrations by Zoe Eggleton and Belinda Clune

All rights reserved. No part of this publication may be reproduced, stored in a retrieval system, or transmitted in any form or by any means (electronic, mechanical, photocopying or otherwise), without the prior written permission of both the copyright owner and the publisher of this book.

To Sasha

May these techniques and ideas
last you a lifetime.

About The Author

Karen Tui Boyes is a champion for Life Long Learning across nations, industries and organisations. She is an author and the creator of the Teachers Matter Conference, Teachers Matter Magazine, Kids Matter Conference, the Study Smart Method, Study Smart Workshops and the Habits of Mind Bootcamp. She is also CEO of Spectrum Education, Affiliate Director of the Institute for the Habits of Mind, NZ Educator of the Year 2017 & 2014, NZ Speaker of the Year 2013, NZ Business Woman of the Year 2001, wife of one and mother of two.

A sought after speaker who continually gets rave reviews from audiences around the world, Karen turns the latest educational research into easy-to-implement strategies and techniques. Karen has the rare ability to draw her audience in and keep them enthralled. She is both informative and entertaining, as she passes on her practical solutions for learning, teaching, studying, living, working, communicating and growing more effectively as a person.

Karen creates an environment where it is fun to learn and it is safe to make mistakes. This encourages participants to be relaxed and totally involved and is proven to produce outstanding results. Karen uses a unique blend of music, colour, games, stories and activities, giving students a mixture of learning tools and an improved self-awareness. Using this new information maximises the yearn-to-learn and the ability to recall and retain information. Thousands of students throughout Australasia have benefited from these techniques and have gone on to score well beyond what they thought they were capable of at exam time.

At the corporate level, Karen works in the areas of motivation, effective communication and attaining and maintaining peak performance. Together these create a friendly, fun environment where superior results are achieved by working smarter rather than harder, with less stress and increased team work.

Table Of Contents

About The Author v
Introduction ix
Learning Styles 1
Study Environment 21
Fast Recall 31
Memory 39
Effective Notes 55
Motivation 65
Rapid Reading 75
Success And Mistakes 87
Goal Setting 93
Time Management 101
Exam Techniques 111
Final Thoughts 117
Bibliography 121
Acknowledgements 123

Introduction

Your ability to learn is probably the most sustainable advantage you'll have in the future.

The word failure is not a pleasant word for most people— especially when it is to do with learning. In fact, the fear of failure is one of the top ten fears.

However you and I as human beings are designed to learn by trial and error—to learn from our mistakes. I believe there is only one failure in life.

The only FAILURE is the FAILURE to ...PARTICIPATE

If you're not participating, you won't make any mistakes.

If you're not making mistakes, you can't be learning.

No one ever told me this when I was at school. I used to go home and study everything I knew. That's not learning— it's revising. Learning is learning— learning is understanding and remembering what you don't know.

When you get a test assignment back and your mark is seven out of ten, you should celebrate. What is the most important part of this mark? The three that you got wrong. This tells you what you still need to learn. The seven tells you what you already know. If you thought the fact that you'd passed was the most important part of the seven out of ten, think again. I'm not sure who decided 50% is a pass, but in the 21st Century this is not enough. Let's say you're employed as an air-traffic controller. Your job is to safely land the planes. After your first day at work you go home and tell your partner, "Honey I passed today. I landed 60% of my planes!" If you're an air traffic controller, 99.9% is not enough! You have to be 100% accurate. Imagine you are going into the hospital for surgery and the doctor thought 80% accuracy was enough! You are not likely to want to go for the operation. The 21st Century demands that we make mistakes, learn from them and get better and better at what we do.

Study Tip
Learn the information
I don't know

Go back over all your tests, assignments and exams and learn what you got wrong. Now this sounds simple, yet most people don't do it. They don't learn the information they got wrong because it's too hard.

Study Tip
Everything is hard before it is easy

However, everything is hard before it is easy. Have you ever watched a young child learn to walk? They stand up, wobble, fall down, cry and get back up. Have you ever heard a mother say to her child, "You've fallen over too many times. You're a failure at walking, so stop trying!" No, of course not. No mother would ever say this, no matter how long it takes to learn to walk.

Here is a simple success formula. This is why everyone, who is physically able to, can walk. When they fell down, they simply got back up. That's it—it's not rocket science— just a simple rule in life to remember. When you fall down, you simply get back up. So learning the information you don't know might be hard to start with, but the more you do it, the easier it will get.

Sometimes, when people make mistakes or get things wrong, certain behaviours can arise that are not useful for continuing the learning process. For example, some people may deny what is happening and pretend it's not their fault or not happening at all. They might pretend that their study is going well and pretend not to notice that they are failing their subjects.

Another behaviour is to make excuses for the results they are getting. For example, making an excuse for not handing in an assignment when the truth is they didn't prioritise the assignment or care enough about completing it.

The third behaviour that often occurs is blaming others for results. A student might say, "It's my teacher's fault I failed the exam", or "It's the government's fault I don't have a job".

These three behaviours keep people from playing the game of life by joining them up to what I call the *Victim Team* (being a victim of life). The good news is there are three alternative behaviours to choose "above the line of life".

The first is to take OWNERSHIP. You can do this simply by saying, "Oops I made a mistake," and admitting you are at fault.

The second is to be ACCOUNTABLE for your life and your results. This means you are able to account for what is happening in your life and why.

The third is a word you probably hear more and more as you're getting older. RESPONSIBILITY. This means taking full responsibility for the results you get without making excuses or blaming others.

People who use these three behaviours play the game of life in what I call the *Learning Team*. I started this book with a quote about your ability to learn being the sustainable advantage in the future. Life in the 21st Century is changing so fast.

Throughout the world there are many classes of seven year olds who, on a daily basis, update and program their own websites and daily blog. Do you have a website or blog? Can you program or update one? These children will have your jobs because they are keeping up with fast technological changes.

Current statistics show that, on average, you will have 10–14 different careers before you are 35 years old—not jobs, but careers. If you decide to train to work as an engineer, it takes four years to train at University. By the time you have been in the workforce for two years, up to 60% of what was taught at University is obsolete. In the field of biotechnology, it takes only one year for half of what you learn to be outdated.

And recent statistics show that every 10 months in the medical field, 50% of information has changed.

Again, your ability to learn and learn from your mistakes is paramount to your success. Not just in school and study, but in life.

As you read and learn the information in this book, note that one of the guarantees I give, that I also give on my seminars, is that if you use at least four of these techniques, you will increase your marks. I also guarantee another thing. If you don't use these ideas and tips, they won't work and if you do use them, they will. Just like learning to ride a bike, the new skills and techniques may be a bit wobbly at first, but the more you persevere and practice the easier they will become.

Some people read a book such as this and then announce that it doesn't work. This is being on the *Victim Team*, below the line of life. It's usually an excuse for not using the techniques or being persistent. At Spectrum Education, we've had over 35,000 students complete our one or two-day study workshops with incredible results.

Study Smart

Learning Team

Ownership
Accountable
Responsible

                                                        Line of Life

Victim Team
Blame
Excuse
Deny

These are just some of the results

- A 17 year old boy increased his chemistry mark from 43% to 76% by simply using baroque music to study with.
- When a 16 year old girl started using colour and mindmapping her notes, her marks went from Bs to As.
- When a 15 year old student realised what sort of learner he was, and studied accordingly, his marks almost doubled in all subjects.
- A university law student's reading speed increased from 257 words per minute to over 1000 words per minute with full comprehension by practising a 16-minute drill daily. This allowed him to read faster and decrease his study time.

Of course not all the techniques and tips in this book will be as useful for you. It's your responsibility to work out what works best for you. However, if you use the tips for at least 30 days, you will start seeing the benefits.

Enjoy learning and **Study Smart**!

Rainbows and Sunshine

Karen

Learning Styles

How you learn, and how you actually absorb information, is a very important part of your learning. It is an equally important part of how you study.

There are five different learning styles—visual, auditory, kinesthetic, olfactory and gustatory. (Bandler & Grinder, 1991) It is important to note that we all display all of these characteristics some of the time. According to authors of *How Your Child is Smart*, Anne Powell and Dawna Markova, it is the combination of these styles that has the biggest affect to your results. Your individual learning style can also change according to many different factors.

As you read through the characteristics of each style, please remember you are all styles and most people have a dominant learning style or one that they prefer. Read through the following information, and think about your behaviour and the behaviour of those around you. You can work out your learning style, as well as that of family members and friends, just by observation.

The Study Tips associated with each learning style can and should be used by all learner types.

> We learn 10% of what we read,
> 15% of what we hear and
> 80% of what we experience.
> **Gordon Dryden**

VISUAL LEARNERS

Visual learners learn by watching and noticing. If you are a visual learner, you will typically sit up straight and watch the teacher's every move. You are most likely to be considered a 'good' learner as you pay attention more often.

Visual Characteristics

- sit up straight
- follow the teacher with their eyes
- speak quickly
- are good long-range planners and organisers

- are appearance-oriented in both dress and presentation
- are good spellers and can actually see the words in their minds
- memorise by visual association
- are not usually distracted by noise
- are neat and orderly
- would rather do a demonstration than make a speech
- like art more than music
- often know what to say but can't think of the right words
- sometimes tune out when they mean to pay attention
- forget to relay verbal messages to others
- have trouble remembering verbal instructions such as directions unless they are written down
- are strong, fast readers

> Your brain can keep learning from birth till the end of life.
> **Marian Diamond**

Study Tip
Use lots of colour

Using colour in your note taking and when you study will increase your ability to remember and recall your information. When you use only one colour, traditionally blue or black, it is called monotone, or monotonous or boring for your brain. Your notes are then boring to reread or study. Using lots of colour ensures that your notes look inviting for rereading and learning. Colour is also processed right next to the part of the brain that stores long term memory. Information in colour is therefore more likely to be remembered.

Use your favourite colours, highlight key information and write on coloured paper. Use felt pens of different thickness to make note taking more interesting and more fun.

AUDITORY LEARNERS

Auditory learners learn by listening and discussing. If you are an auditory learner, you may gaze out the classroom window, but you'll be listening carefully. You might sometimes find it distracting to look at the same time as you are listening.

> Percentage of what is remembered when we:
>
> Read—20%
>
> Hear—30%
>
> See—40%
>
> Say—50%
>
> Do—60%
>
> See, say, hear and do—90%
>
> **Dr Vernon Magnesen**

Auditory Characteristics

- speak rhythmically
- follow the speaker with the ear
- can repeat back and mimic tone, pitch and timbre
- remember what was said, word for word, six weeks earlier
- are good at imitating voices
- talk to themselves while working
- are easily distracted by noise
- move their lips and pronounce words as they read

- enjoy reading aloud and listening to stories
- find writing difficult and are better at telling
- are frequently eloquent speakers
- learn by listening and remembering what was discussed
- are talkative, love discussion and go into lengthy descriptions
- spell better out loud than in written form
- are good at remembering and telling jokes

> **Study Tip**
> Talk about your information

Talk about your information as much as possible. When you say information out loud it is reinforced in your brain. Have you ever asked someone to remind you to do something? Do they usually need to remind you? Not usually. When you say something out loud it comes out of your mouth and goes back in through your ears into your long term memory.

Learning Styles

Karena & Kirsten's Story

Two friends of mine used the "Talk about your information" Study Tip to great advantage while studying at University. Karena was studying Molecular Biology while Kirsten was in her final year of Criminology. Most evenings while studying the two would discuss what they were learning. By the end of the year, not only did they know their own information well, they also knew each other's. They often laugh about how they could have sat each other's exams and still passed with A's.

Talk about your study notes and what you are learning with a friend or even to yourself out loud. You'll be amazed at how the information sticks. Teaching someone about your subject is also a useful strategy. You could even tell or teach your younger brother or sister, or your parents, the important information you are learning. Finding a study buddy, someone you can discuss your study notes with, is also useful.

KINESTHETIC LEARNERS

There are two types of kinesthetic learners—tactile/movement-oriented learners and feeling-oriented learners. If you are a tactile/movement learner, you will fidget and wriggle. You will want to touch anything and everything. If you are a feeling kinesthetic learner you will be involved with your own feelings. You will want to be comfortable and feel loved and safe. You will enjoy lying on the floor or on a soft cushion while working.

Kinesthetic Tactile Characteristics

- speak slowly and loudly
- are challenged by sitting still
- respond to physical rewards
- touch people to get their attention
- stand close when talking to someone
- are physically oriented and move a lot
- learn by manipulating and doing
- memorise by walking and seeing
- use a finger as a pointer when reading

- gesture a lot
- remember geography when they have actually been there
- may have messy handwriting
- want to act things out
- like involved games

> Every human being has a learning style
> and every human being has strengths.
> **Ken & Rita Dunn**

Kinesthetic Feeling Characteristics

- dress for comfort
- slouch in their chairs
- prefer to sit or lay on the floor
- are quick to notice temperature changes
- may like to read/work under the tables as this gives them a feeling of safety and warmth

Study Tip
Move around while you're learning

Many people like to move around while they're learning. Moving around or not sitting still has many advantages. It increases blood flow allowing more oxygen to the brain, therefore making learning easier. Get up while you're studying and move around at least every 20 minutes. Walk around while you're reading. Sit on an exercycle or mini tramp while you're studying. Fiddle with a koosh ball or some blu tack. Doodle on your page while you're listening. Nod your head and wriggle your toes when sitting for long periods of time. Nodding helps to keep the blood flowing and is also useful if moving around in class annoys your teacher.

> To succeed you must be
> easy to start and hard to stop.
> **Bob Pike**

Study Tip
Frame important information

Research at the International Accelerated Learning Conference in 1998 showed framing work can increase test scores. Simply by putting a frame around information, your brain focuses within the frame. If there is no frame, your focus is anywhere. Frame all important work. If you are a doodler, I suggest you doodle frames around your pages in class to help you concentrate and raise your understanding of what's in the frame.

OLFACTORY LEARNING

Olfactory is the sense of smell. When you walk into a room the first thing you notice, subconsciously, is the temperature. The second thing you notice, again subconsciously, is the smell. What do you typically find right next to the door of a classroom? Yes, the rubbish bin. So what messages do you think you get subconsciously whenever you walk into a classroom? This stinks, this is rubbish! In your study environment, it is very important to have good, positive smells that will make it more pleasant, and easier for your learning.

Aromatherapy Oils:

Basil

An excellent oil to aid concentration and relieve mental fatigue. It is focusing, reviving, stimulating and strengthening.

Rosemary

For mental exhaustion and memory recall. It is stimulating, focusing, clearing and activating.

Lemon

A great oil to encourage mental alertness and relieve nervous tension. It is uplifting, cleansing, clearing and refreshing.

Peppermint

Excellent to rouse the mind, promote mental clarity and relieve nervous stress. It is cooling, soothing, refreshing and stimulating.

Lavender

Is the great leveller. It can create calm and order, harmonise and balance. It is relaxing, calming, nurturing and comforting.

Kim Morrison, co-author of Like Chocolate For Women–Indulge and Recharge with Everyday Aromatherapy says, the reason a pleasant smell makes it easier for your learning is that when the five senses come into your brain, they go through a place called the thalamus. (Hannaford, 1995) The thalamus is like a transfer station. Sight comes in through your eyes, into the thalamus which sends it to the occipital lobes at the back of your head to process. Sound comes in through your ears, into the thalamus, and the thalamus shifts it over into the temporal lobes at the side of your head to process. This happens for every sense, except smell.

When the nose identifies a smell it travels up the nasal cavity where millions of olfactory sensors are located. These sensors send messages to the brain via the emotional centre of the brain. Within four seconds of registering an odour the brain releases chemicals and endorphins into the body causing an emotional or physical reaction.

The area of the brain which registers smell is very closely linked to the area where your long term memory is stored.

Have you ever walked past someone, smelled their perfume, and instantly remembered someone who used to smell like that? This is the long term memory. The smell of grandmother's cooking will trigger memory directly because the smell has gone straight into your long term memory.

Certain oils such as Basil, Rosemary, Lemon and Peppermint are classified as stimulants or cephalic (able to help stimulate and clear the mind). A bath with five or six drops of Rosemary is wonderful if you have woken exhausted in the morning. Inhaling a drop of

Peppermint on a tissue is a great 'I'm awake now' oil! A blend of six drops in total, two drops each of Basil, Rosemary and Lemon into your vaporiser or one drop of each on a tissue is an excellent way to help increase your retention and memory. Take your aromatic tissue using these oils, in to an exam with you. Before reading the first page of questions, take three deep breaths holding your aromatic tissue. This will help alleviate nerves, calm your diaphragm and evoke easier recall and memory. The smell of these oils will instantly take you to the place of studying where you had no pressure and your books open.

Lavender is a highly recommended oil to relieve stress and promote relaxation and sleep after a full day learning— study or being at the computer. A bath with six drops of Lavender before bed is a brilliant way to switch off before sleep. A single drop of Lavender on a tissue and placed under your pillow will help encourage and promote a good night's sleep. Aromatherapy can be that easy and powerful.

GUSTATORY LEARNING

Gustatory learning concerns your sense of taste. Children's blood sugar levels cycle about every 45 minutes. In adults, it's every 90 minutes and in teenagers, about every 60 minutes. When your blood sugar levels are low, learning is very difficult. Keeping your blood sugar levels up is important for keeping on learning. However, what you eat is almost more important. There are good foods for your brain and memory, and there are bad foods.

Study Tip
When studying, eat brain food at least once an hour

What is brain food?

To begin with, the best food for your brain is protein. The best sources of protein are unsalted nuts, chicken and fish. Fish, for many years, has been called brain food. Fish contains essential oils and amino acids that your brain uses directly. I'm not talking about the processed "fish and chips" fish, or takeaway chicken, but fresh fish and chicken.

Sometimes takeaway food looks quick and easy and even tastes good. On February 27th 2002 I purchased a McDonalds cheeseburger. I left it on a plate in my office. To this day over 16 years later, this burger looks the same as the day I purchased it. The bread, cheese and meat hasn't gone mouldy.

Another food group that is good for your brain is fruit and vegetables. Essentially, what your brain needs from fruit and vegetables is vitamin B and vitamin C. If you're not getting enough vitamins B or C, you may find it a little harder to remember things. In fact, research shows that when elderly people supplemented their diets with vitamins B and C, their memory recall went up 100%. (Ward & Daley, 1993)

There is one other food that is absolutely fantastic for the brain, and you can eat as much of this as you like — popcorn. Popcorn is a complex carbohydrate giving you lots of energy without the sugar rush. It is best eaten plain and unsalted.

Study Tip
Drink at least 6-8 glasses of water a day

WATER

Approximately 70% of our bodies are made up of water and over 80% of our brains consist of water. Not enough water can lead to dehydration which causes headaches, lack of concentration and focus, and tiredness. Drinking at least six to eight glasses of water a day is important for health and success. At any time of stress the body dehydrates. Have you ever stood up in front of a group to speak and your mouth suddenly goes dry? According to Dr Batmanghelidj (1997), the 'dry mouth' signal is the last outward sign of extreme dehydration. Dr Carla Hannaford (1995) suggests under any stress the body needs two to three times the normal daily amount of water.

Keep a water bottle beside you when you study and take water into the exam with you if you are allowed. Drink between classes. You do not need to be sucking on a drink bottle continuously in class. Just ensure you rehydrate between classes.

What should I avoid?
Sugar

Sugar creates an addiction cycle in your body that makes your brain work overtime. When you eat something sweet, your body starts to pump adrenaline and you feel good. However while your body is using the sugar, your pancreas produces insulin to bring your body back into balance. This makes you feel worse than you did before eating the sugar. Then you think you need something else sweet to eat, and suddenly you've set up an addiction cycle. It's particularly detrimental for you around exam time and when you're studying because your brain focuses on the need for more sugar, rather than the fact that you need to sit down and study. Avoiding sugar at study and exam time is important.

Caffeine

Caffeine is found in tea, coffee, coke and other soft drinks, cigarettes and chocolate. Smart drinks also contain caffeine. Caffeine is a diuretic and this means each cup or glass of a drink containing caffeine dehydrates your body of up to three glasses of water. You may have a cup of coffee and then feel quite thirsty. You have another cup of coffee, become even more thirsty and have another cup of coffee. Dr Batmanghelidj, in his book Your Body's Many Cries For Water states, "It's an elementary but catastrophic mistake to think caffeine drinks are a substitute for water." He continues to say, "It's true they contain water, but they also contain dehydration agents and use the water they are dissolved in as well as the reserves from the body." Around exam and study time, avoid caffeine as much as possible.

> Brain functioning depends very much on what you've eaten for breakfast.
> **Richard M Restak**

Artificial Sweetener (951)

Artificial sweeteners in diet drinks, diet products and chewing gum are a leading cause ofx mental fatigue as well as MS, Parkinson disease and diabetes. (Kedgley, 1998) In many countries, the sweetener 951 (aspartame) is a banned substance. You are better to have the sugar and exercise it off.

MSG—Mono Sodium Glutamate

MSG is a flavour enhancer in food (labelled as flavour enhancer 621 on food packaging). It's also a leading cause of mental fatigue. MSG has been linked to very poor brain development in children. It speeds up your brain, making it work far too fast for learning. Avoid it, if possible, when you're studying.

> A journey of a thousand miles must begin with a single step.
>
> **Lao Tze**

Study Environment

If you want your learning to be as effective as possible, you need to plan your physical environment carefully. Much organisation and planning goes into something such as a musical performance or a birthday party, and the same amount of planning should go into making your study environment excellent for learning. Just as you consider factors such as lighting, music, costumes, rehearsals, venue, food and drink when planning a performance or a party, you should also think about them when you're planning your study.

Study Tip
Study with low lighting

Lighting

Lighting shouldn't be too bright in your study area. Bright light reflecting off a white page can stress your eyes and make learning harder. Dr Rita Dunn's research shows that for 70% of students, studying with low lighting is best. Did you ever read under the bed covers when you were very young? Your parents probably told you you'd ruin your eyesight, but this isn't true. For most children and teenagers, low lighting is the most effective. In fact, as we get older, into our mid-20s, our eye muscles start to weaken and we need brighter light and sometimes glasses. If possible, avoid fluorescent lights as these flicker at a different rate than your brain and interrupt brain processing. They can cause tiredness, lack of motivation and even headaches.

> **Study Tip**
> Study to music
> without words

Music

Some people prefer to study in silence, while others prefer to study with music in the background. If you study to music with words, your brain will focus on the words and not on what you are learning. Instrumental tracks of your favourite music will also not be useful because your brain is likely to still put the words in.

Finding somewhere silent can be quite difficult in today's busy world. There's nearly always something going on in the background — traffic noise, the neighbour's lawnmower or conversations between other family members. Here are two ways to create complete silence in your study environment. Buy yourself a pair of earmuffs, the kind people wear when they're mowing the lawns. If you are wearing earmuffs, however, you should let someone know what you're doing so they can come and get you in case of an emergency, like a house fire. Many people use ear plugs at university while studying in the library. This creates a quiet space and less auditory distractions.

If you like to study with some background music, the type you choose is very important. Specifically, Baroque music is the most useful. This is because it has sixty beats per minute which is equivalent to your resting heart rate and accesses your long term memory.

Baroque Composers:
Bach, Handel, Pachelbel, Vivaldi, Telemann, Albinoni, Purcell, Gluck, Corelli

An interesting study quoted in Colin Rose's book

Accelerating Learning on music and silence was completed by Mrs Rettallack of Denver, where she set up three identical rooms full of plants. In the first room, there was complete silence. The second room was filled with loud rock music for the three months and the third room had baroque music pumped in. At the end of the three months, the plants that were in complete silence were still just normal healthy plants. The plants with the rock music were shrivelled and dying, and the plants with the baroque music were flourishing and growing more than anyone had thought possible.

What was even more amazing about this room was that every single plant in the room was growing towards the speakers. Now, your brain isn't a plant, but if this kind of music enhances plant growth, maybe it also enhances brain function. You don't have to listen to this kind of music all the time but it can be very, useful when studying.

Tom's Story

A 15 year old student, Tom, who attended Spectrum's two day Super Student workshop learned about the power of Baroque Music and study. He downloaded a couple Baroque playlists. Initially he played it really loud, but soon turned it down so that it was quiet background music. After several weeks of studying with the music in the background he was overheard saying, "I hate that music—but it works!" He continues to play the music two years later and is achieving fabulous results.

In fact while I was writing this book I had a Baroque music playing quietly in the background. It helped keep me focused for three months.

Study Tip
Play Baroque music quietly in
the background while studying

If you're studying maths or learning a new language, listening to Mozart's music can be very helpful. Gordon Shaw from the Californian University in Irvine has scientifically proven that listening to Mozart for ten minutes will increase your ability to learn maths and a new language for approximately thirty minutes.

Study Tip
Wear comfortable clothes
during exams

Clothing

Wearing comfortable clothes sounds so obvious and simple and many people don't do it. If you wear your school uniform, make sure you have a jersey or a jacket with you as the room may get cold. Remember, you're in an exam for up to three hours, the weather can change quickly and you can suddenly get hot or cold. If your clothing is tight or uncomfortable you can very quickly lose focus. You will be thinking about how uncomfortable you are and you won't be able to concentrate. Wear comfortable, loose clothing when you're studying and also during your exams.

A great tip a student once gave me was to use your jacket or jersey to sit on during an exam. It makes those hard chairs a bit more comfortable.

> ## Study Tip
> Practise old exam papers

Rehearsal

Rehearsal is one of the most important aspects of studying. Practise and practise old exam & test papers. It may take three or four weeks to complete them. Make sure you get someone to check the answers for you so that you can learn from the questions you got wrong.

Many scientists believe that studying just before you go to sleep is the most beneficial time as this is when you are accessing your long term memory.

Karen's Story

Practising old exam papers is one of the key techniques that really got me through my second year of exams. My midyear chemistry mark was 27% which wasn't too good and indicated that I had more work to do if I wanted to pass chemistry. So, I found all the old exam papers I could. (I went to the school library, my chemistry teacher and asked students who had sat the paper the previous year for copies of old papers. You can now download them from the internet.) I practised and practised these exam papers, and I discovered something very interesting. Because there is a curriculum for chemistry (and, of course all other subjects), and you are tested on the curriculum, the information you are tested on is often the same every year. In fact, sometimes the questions in exam papers are the same. The most amazing thing for me though, was that when I actually sat my chemistry exam there were two questions that I had already done because they had just been taken straight from a past paper. Often you will find that certain questions are repeated, especially in English exams where the same format is followed year after year. I ended up getting 83% for chemistry and all because I went over and over and over past papers. One important thing to remember here is that when you practise the exam paper, please make sure you get someone to check the answers so that you can find out which questions you're answering correctly and which ones you need help with.

Study Tip
Practise writing before an exam

When you sit your exams, you may be writing solidly for up to three hours. Make sure your muscles are up to it, and if necessary, practise writing solidly for an hour or more at a time in the weeks leading up to your exams. This is especially true if you are used to typing rather than writing. You want your hands and arms to be able to keep up with your brain! It is easier for the brain to read lower case letters than capitals. This is why books and newspapers are not written in CAPITALS. When learning important information, use lower case letters as often as possible.

Karen's Writing Tip

About six weeks before an exam I start to build up the muscles in my writing hand so that I don't get sore hands or cramps. If I was an athlete I would go to the gym to build up my muscles so its a similar thing to build up your muscles for writing. What I do is spend about an hour, two or three times a week, writing solidly. I might write to some friends, I might write out the words to my favourite songs or my favourite book. If an hour is too long, start with half an hour. A few weeks before the exam I double the amount of time that I spend writing so that by the time I get to the exam the muscles are stronger, I can write quickly and my arm can keep up with my brain.

Study Tip
Study at your best thinking time

Time of Day

Are you a morning, afternoon or evening person? Study when you are most alert. If you are a morning person, get up an hour earlier than normal and study then. If you prefer to stay up late at night, study during this time. Make sure you study in a place where you're not going to be disturbed.

You may prefer to study at a desk or a table, or you might lie on the floor or on your bed when you study. If you do this, here's a word of warning. Avoid lying in the same position as you do when you're sleeping. If you do, you are likely to fall asleep. You might like to study outside. Take your notes with you to the nearest park, riverside or beach. You might like to study in the shower. (I know people who do this!) Write your notes out, laminate them or put them in a plastic bag and blu-tack them high up in the shower. Read them while you're shampooing. Use plenty of colour in your notes. You'll not only be able to see them more clearly through the water, but the colour will help you remember more. The worst time to study is one hour straight after school. Remember to take time after school to refresh and relax for an hour and then complete homework, assignments and study.

> **Study Tip**
> Get everything ready before
> you begin studying

Preparation

Get everything you need ready before you sit down to begin your study. Otherwise you will have countless interruptions. Get all your books, pens, pencils and paper together. Also, get yourself a glass of water that you can sip while you study. You could even have a snack, such as nuts or fruit handy so you can study uninterrupted.

Keep Your Energy Level High

Deep breathing, neck exercises and an upright spine all allow blood, oxygen and energy to pass freely between body and brain.

Study Tip
Do exam aerobics

Exercise

Sitting for three hours can become very uncomfortable. Also, the blood in your body can start to pool in your ankles. As blood is the carrier of oxygen to your brain, you need to keep it moving around your body. Keep yourself moving in the exam to keep your blood flowing around your body. Move your ankles, roll your shoulders backwards and forward, tense your muscles and relax them, stretch your arms towards the ceiling. You can do these exercises without disturbing anyone else in the exam.

3

Fast Recall

In this chapter you'll discover how your brain processes information and how you can use this information to learn faster, recall faster and retain what you've learnt – forever, if you want. In fact the techniques described in this section are the most popular from Spectrum's two day Super Student workshop and can also produce a huge rise in your marks.

You may have heard the saying, "Your eyes are the window to your soul". Your eyes are also the window to your brain. Research shows that when you look up, you're accessing your visual memory, what you've seen and what things look like. When you look sideways, you are accessing your auditory channel—the listening and hearing. When you look down and to the left, you are accessing the self-talk channel, the little voice inside your head, talking to yourself. When you look down and to the right, you are accessing your feelings. (Knight, 1995)

Eye Movements

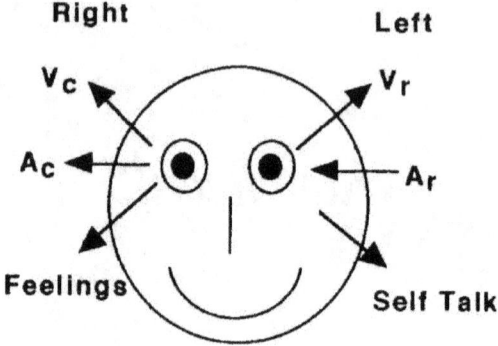

Vc—Visual construct
Vr—Visual recall
Ac—Auditory construct
Ar—Auditory recall

Have you ever noticed where people look when they cry? Usually down and often to the right because they are accessing their feelings. Crying is an important emotion. However, there are times when it's not OK to cry or times when you want to stop someone crying. If you want to stop yourself from crying, all you have to do is look up. You can no longer access your feelings when you're looking up.

EYE-WATCHING EXERCISE

Sit across from another person. Ask this person the following questions and watch their eyes as they answer you:

• **How many windows are there in your house?**

Watch where their eyes go. If their eyes go up, you can't tell what they are thinking, but you can tell how they are processing the information. You know that they have some sort of picture inside their head. They may be thinking, "What does my house look like?" They are looking for it. If their eyes go sideways, you still can't tell what they are thinking, but you can tell how they are processing. They are saying to themselves something like, "I remember a conversation about windows." If their eyes go down to the right, they are probably feeling, "Gee, I hate washing windows." or "I feel silly doing this."

- **What would you look like with purple hair, elephant ears and a green tongue?**

Watch their eyes. If their eyes go up, you know they are thinking some kind of visual picture. If they go sideways, they are saying something inside their head. If they go down to the right, they are feeling something like, "Gee, I look horrible."

Karen's Example

Have you ever had a baby-sitting job? When I was 16 I was baby-sitting for one of my teachers from school. At 7 o'clock I said to Susan wtho was six, "OK, it's time to go to bed", and off she went. Then I said to three-year-old Jake, "OK Jake, time for bed." I got him into bed but he started to cry. And he cried and he cried and he cried. At one o'clock in the morning he was still crying. I tried everything I could think of including phoning my parents for some advice, but nothing stopped this boy from crying. Finally, at 1am in the morning in desperation I phoned his parents and said, "Jake's crying and I can't stop him. Please come home." I'm sure you can guess what Jake was doing when his parents got home! Yes, sitting up in bed smiling. I felt very, very stupid. If only I had known—to stop someone crying, just get them to look up. It's so simple. You can no longer access your feelings when you're looking up.

- **What was the very first thing you said this morning?**

This time you might see their eyes going further sideways as they rewind the day and everything they said, just like rewinding a cassette tape.

Visual, auditory and kinesthetic information is processed at different neurological speeds in the brain. Let's take a look at how this works. Look at a poster or picture on the wall. Close your eyes and notice how long the actual picture lasts for, not the reconstructed one that you make up in your head, but the actual picture. How long did the image last? A split second and then it is gone.

Clap your hands and listen to the sound. Does the sound last longer than the image of the picture? A little bit longer. This means that it takes a little bit longer for the brain to process the sound.

Lastly, clap your hands together as hard as you can. Notice how long that sensation lasts. Longer still? Kinesthetic processing takes a little bit longer. An example of this is the fact that strong kinesthetic learners tend to talk a little bit slower than other learners. This is not because they are less intelligent. It is because it takes just a little bit longer to process the information. Another example is the strong visual learner who talks very quickly. This is because there is a picture inside their head and all they want to do is get the picture out so they process information quickly.

How do we actually use this information then? Let's look at a skill such as spelling. Some people are good spellers, others are creative spellers. Creative spelling is spelling that is different from the dictionary. The only difference between being good at spelling and being creative is the way you use your neurology, the way you use your eyes and how you process the information.

Is spelling in the English language a visual, auditory or kinesthetic skill? If English was an auditory language, we would spell "enuf" like this, as it sounds. There are hundreds of other words in the English language that are spelt differently from how they sound—nite, fone etc. The English language is not, predominantly, an auditory language. It is a visual language. It doesn't matter how many times you say e-nuu-ff, you will never get it right unless you know what it looks like. You have to know exactly how it looks to get it right.

The Maori language (and many other languages), on the other hand, is an auditory language. You can spell almost any Maori word by writing it down the way it sounds.

If visual processing is your fastest memory recall, it is the best to use to study and recall information in an exam. This technique is called eidetic memory or photographic memory. Ninety five percent of five-year-olds have a photographic memory, yet it is extremely rare in adulthood. One reason for this is because you simply haven't continued to practice it. There are four simple steps to a photographic memory. Use these steps to remember dates, formulas, the plot of a play, words in another language etc. When you get good at this you can use this technique to recall whole pages of information.

Step 1

Write a date or a formula or something you need to learn on a card. Hold the card at eye level and then lift it higher until you're looking up as high as you can. Keep looking at the card, and keep your chin down, just look up with your eyes.

Step 2

Look at the card, close your eyes and use your brain like a camera—taking a photo of the word and developing the photo in your mind. Open your eyes, look at the card, close your eyes, open your eyes, look at the card, close your eyes, open, close, open, close, open, close. Almost flutter your eyelashes at this card. Why? Because your brain needs to see a new word or a concept approximately 300-400 times before it knows it off by heart. This puts the information into your visual memory. It's no coincidence that 95% of 4-year-olds know the words McDonalds, Coca Cola, The Warehouse, Exit and Nickelodeon. Why do they know these words? They see them often, but where do they see them? Up high. They are looking up to see them so they learn them quickly.

Step 3

Close your eyes and look up. This is a funny feeling. Can you see the word or information? If not repeat steps 1 and 2 until you can.

Step 4

Recall the word or information forwards and backwards. The only purpose for checking if you can see it backwards is to check that the information is in your visual, fast recall memory.

> Use this technique for remembering dates and formulas, write your information in different colours to stimulate your memory.
>
> Step 1 • Look Up
> Step 2 • Blink 40 times
> Step 3 • Close your eyes and look up
> Step 4 • Recall the information forwards and backwards

Success Stories

A student in Hamilton stuck all her important study notes high around the toilet walls with bluetack. Not only did she learn all her information, her 12 year old brother also learned it! What else was he going to do while sitting there? Even her mother knew all the information, without even trying.

Now I'm not suggesting you have to study in the toilet, although the technique worked for this student!

Another student from Napier used this technique at University. He attached ropes high across his bedroom ceiling and hung all his study notes from the ropes. To study he would simply sit in a different place in the room and look up. He passed every exam.

Study Tip
Put all information up high

Study Tip
When you can't remember something, look up

You are allowed to look up in an exam to access information from your memory. What you are not allowed to do, is look at anyone else's work! If you can't recall information, put your eyes in the right place to access the information, look up and imagine seeing the information written in your study notes and in your books.

> The harder you work the luckier you get.
> **Gary Player**

Memory

Now is an exciting time to be living as far as our brain potential is concerned. For the first time in history, researchers are discovering how our brains work. A new science has emerged within the past fifteen years: Cognomics, the study of how the brain works. (Sousa, 2001) With new technology scientists are able to follow exactly what is happening inside your head. Using this information and knowledge we now know some of the best ways to use the brain for learning and studying.

Study Tip
Learn your most important
information first

> I have an incredible memory...
> as long as I remember to use it.
> **Rich Allen**

Firsts (Primacy)

Do you remember your first day of school? Do you remember what you were wearing and who you talked to on that day? Do you remember the first time you drove a car? Do you remember your seventh day of school? Or your tenth? Probably not, as these aren't as memorable as the first. Generally, anything that happens first in your life will be more memorable than subsequent times. When you sit down to study, go over your most important information first, as it will

be more memorable for you. If you are not sure what is most important, check with your teachers, lecturers or tutors and remember to learn the data you don't know. Revising your notes from yesterday is a great first at the beginning of your study time.

Study Tip
Revise your most important information last

> There's nothing wrong with your memory—
> you just need to use it properly.
>
> Colin Rose

Lasts (Recency)

Your brain also remembers the last thing that occurs or the most recent times. Which part of a movie do you usually remember? Which part of a novel? Usually the ending. Firsts and lasts are both important for your memory. Here are some interesting statistics. If you read a traditional accelerating learning book it will tell you, quite correctly, that you can be learning for a certain period of time, in a lecture type situation, and then your brain will get full and information recall will get harder. This happens approximately every fifty minutes. These books suggest to study or learn for 50 minutes and then take a ten minute break. However, if you do this, study for 50 minutes and take a ten minute break, how many firsts and lasts do you have in an hour time frame? Two. One at the beginning of the session and another at the end. There are two opportunities for what you are studying to be memorable. However, if you just study a little bit smarter, and study for twenty minutes, then take a five minute break, you would have six firsts and lasts over a one hour period. That means that six times over an hour, it's easier to remember your information.

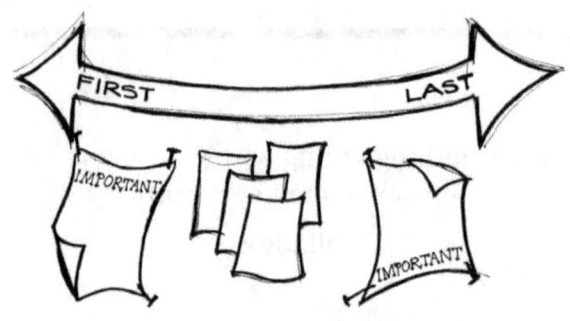

Study Tip
Study for 20 minutes and take a 5 minute break

This tip is especially useful if you're finding your study difficult. If it's going well and you're in a good flow and you're remembering what you are learning, you may not need to take a break. However, if it's hard and beginning to feel like a chore you should take a five minute break, every 20 minutes. During your break, always leave your study area. You could have some brain food, drink some water, or go to the bathroom. During a break from studying, ensure you stretch, like before exercising, as this allows more oxygen into your lungs and therefore more blood and oxygen to your brain—enhancing learning.

Karen's Story

One of the things I do when I'm studying and trying to learn new information that's difficult, is go out to the mailbox every 20 minutes and see if the postie has been. Then I walk back and sit down and continue studying. Twenty minutes later, I'm up again and out to the mailbox. There are two benefits to doing this. Fresh air and exercise. My neighbours must think I am absolutely crazy. Every twenty minutes they see me walk to the letter box. You would be surprised how many times I find something in my mail box!

Download the iStudyAlarm App FREE from the Apple App store or GooglePlay.

> ## Study Tip
> Go over your notes one day after learning them, then one week later, one month later, then every six months

Reviewing

Reviewing is not just repetition. Actively reviewing your notes can at least double your recall. By reading over your mind maps, grabbing your notes and going through

them or talking about and discussing your notes the next day, your recall can stay at 90%. However, if you do not review your notes for three days, your recall will drop to 30%. You will forget 70% of what you have learned in three days without active reviewing. Most information is forgotten because it wasn't moved from your short term memory to your long term memory. Reviewing ensures new information is "installed" into your long term memory.

Make it a priority to revise your notes the very next day to keep them at 90% recall.

If you wish to keep your recall at 90% then you will need to review your notes within 24 hours, then after one week, one month and every six months after that.

An important reminder when reviewing, each topic should only take three or four minutes for review. Only go over your notes and mind maps, not the original book. Only refer to the original source of information if you need clarification of facts, details and information.

Karen's Story

A teacher gave me a great example of the use of repetition by one of her students. This particular student was achieving marks in the 90% range. One day, during class, a student asked her how she always got these high marks. The girl replied, "Each night, after school I write the summary points of each class on a card the size of a postcard. The next day while walking to school, I read the cards so I can remember everything from the day before." She was using the one day repetition.

A great way to review is with a review concert invented by Dr Georgi Lozanov. Simply record your information on your computer or phone, with soft Baroque music playing in the background. Replay this when you are relaxed and just listen.

Using this technique Lozanov was able to teach people to speak a new language, fluently, in six weeks!

Researcher Chris Evans (Rose, 1999) believes the most important function of sleep is to allow you brain to consider the new things that have been learned that day. He suggests new learnings are filed and consolidated in the memory system during sleep. He suggests this review technique.

Review your notes:

- 1 day
- 1 week
- 1 month
- 6 months

Study Tip
Make up stories and mnemonics about your information

Stands Out

Your brain loves anything that is funny, different or has a novelty value. Anything like this will stand out in your mind. Any "one offs" will be memorable. Often the sillier something is, the more memorable it will be. I have strong memories of a teacher who stood on his chair while teaching about height. The same teacher sat under a desk to teach us about earthquakes!

Following are six ways to make important information stand out in your mind.

1. Mnemonics (nem-on-ic) are a way of remembering information. How do you remember the colours of the rainbow? Many people remember the mnemonic ROYGBIV, which stands for Red, Orange, Yellow, Green, Blue, Indigo, Violet.
   If you're doing chemistry you can remember the periodic table by remembering a mnemonic—**H**ow **He** **Li**kes **Be**er **B**y the **C**upfull **N**ot **O**ver **F**rothy. Hydrogen, Helium, Lithium, Beryllium, Boron, Carbon, Nitrogen, Oxygen, Fluorine.
   For reading music—the notes in the spaces spell F, A, C, E and the notes on the lines stand for **E**very **G**ood **B**oy **D**eserves **F**ruit.
   Make up mnemonics about your work.

2. Highlight key points within your notes. If you highlight all your notes they will not stand out anymore. It is important to use many different techniques for making your information stand out.

3. Use the colour red for difficult or important facts. This colour goes straight into your long term memory. Of course if all your notes are in red they won't stand out anymore!

4. Frame key ideas and number the points you're learning. That way you will know if you have recalled all of them.

5. When practising spelling make the bits you need to learn standout such as sepArate repEtition rHythm.

6. Make up rhymes, chants, songs or raps to remember your notes.

> **Study Tip**
> Learn only three or four
> things at a time

Chunking

The adult short term memory can remember between five and nine pieces of information in one chunk. When the brain is given too many pieces of information to remember it installs amnesia or chunks out. To demonstrate this, read the following sequence of numbers, once only, then turn away and write them down.

4, 12, 76, 34, 23, 87, 3, 67, 92, 88, 23, 94, 5, 10

Did you feel your brain go fuzzy? This is what happens when you study too much information at once. This is exactly why cramming for an exam is not effective. Have you ever done this? Shoved all the information in the night before a test or exam only to discover when you sit in the test or exam room, you can remember studying the information, what side of the page it was written on, what you had for dinner, what you were wearing—everything except the exact information you need? This is because you are studying too many pieces of information at once and your brain 'chunks out'. As a rule of thumb, your short term memory can only cope with seven, plus or minus two pieces of information at a time. That's between five and nine pieces of information.

Success Story

Many years ago a student rang me six weeks before an Art History Exam. She was in a panic as she had six weeks to learn 150 paintings. This was a HUGE task. We chunked the task down to four paintings per day, which was more manageable, but still a lot to learn every day. To make this more effective she learned two in the morning and two at night. The following day before learning the next two, she revised everything she had learned so far. The key to her success was not only chunking, she also started with the hard ones first, leaving the easier paintings until closer to the exam. This meant she would go over and over the hard ones, making them easy. (Remember—everything is hard before it is easy.)

By the time she sat the exam, all the paintings were easy, and she passed with 87%!

> **NOTE:** This story does not give you permission to study for only six weeks. She worked extremely hard and had other subjects to learn as well. It is easier to spread the load throughout the year than bust yourself in the last few weeks.

When remembering a telephone number, I often break it into smaller chunks. The smaller, more manageable the chunks, the faster you will pick up the information. Break your study content into small pieces so you find it easy to recall. Learn three or four pieces of data at a time, then revise it, check you can still recall the facts. Then learn three or four more pieces of information, revise these and the last 'chunk'. If you can recall the last chunks, continue this way, always pausing to revisit the previous 'chunks'.

Study Tip
Create real life examples

Association (Linking)

Scientists now understand that new information is stored in the short term memory for 24 hours before it is lost forever. Within this 24 hours it must be linked to information stored in your long term memory. This is called velcro learning. There are two parts to make velcro work. If you only have one part it doesn't work. There are also two parts to making memory work by linking the short term memory with the long term memory. Association or linking is one key to this. Association is putting things together that naturally go together such as cat and dog or chair and table. True learning actually happens when you associate what you are learning with what you already know. It is not being able to pass a test or repeat new data. Learning is when you can use or apply the information in real life. Finding a reason to learn something makes it easier to remember. Have you ever sat in class thinking, I'm going to die one day, why am I learning this?" This is not such a useful question to be asking. Create meaning by asking your teacher, "Why am I learning this?", "How will this be useful?", "What jobs could I go into if I was good at this subject?" If your teacher isn't sure find out for yourself. The more real life examples you can find, the easier the information will be to remember.

Karen's Story

My English Teacher used association to teach essay writing. I learned to write essays using the hamburger method. There are three parts to a hamburger and three parts to an essay.

- The top bun or introduction
- The filling or body of the essay
- The bottom bun or conclusion/summary

An essay without an introduction is an open sandwich not a hamburger. The best part of the hamburger is the filling. The body should be the best part of your essay and the part you spend the most time on. If you leave off the bottom bun when making a hamburger you end up with a mess! Similarly an essay needs a conclusion to hold it all together.

Study Tip
Draw pictures and diagrams

Visuals

Pictures are located in the same part of the brain as the long term memory. When you're studying, turn your key concepts into pictures. The first picture you draw or think of is usually the most memorable. The sillier the picture, the better it is for remembering as it stands out. Colourful pictures are often easier to remember. Your visuals can be imagined, drawn or made. If you can't draw a picture such as with dates or words in a foreign language, write them large and in colour. Your brain will process this as a picture not a word. Remember to put key information up high so your fast visual recall memory processes it.

Flash Cards

Flash cards are also useful. If you are learning words in another language, write the foreign word on one side if the card and the English word on the reverse. Test yourself with both sides of the cards—first in English then in the foreign language. Remember to make piles of the easy and hard ones so you can practice the hard ones more often.

> There is always a better way to do it — find it.
> Thomas Edison

Memory Flashing

Use a memory flashing technique similar to the repeat, repeat mind map process. Look at the information you want to recall. Turn the page upside down or close your book so you can't see the information. Next rewrite it from memory. Check to see if you remembered it all. Repeat several times, until you know it, remembering to place special attention to the data or ideas you didn't recall and learning these. Of course it is important to review it the next day and a week later to check you still can recall it.

Jigsaw cards

These are a fun kinesthetic visual way of learning. Write a question and answer on either end of a strip of paper or card. Cut the card in half with a jigsaw cut, ensuring the question is on one half and answer on the other.

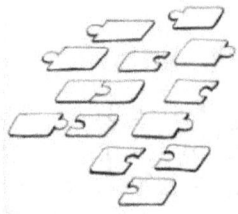

Practice putting the piece back together paying special attention to the information on the cards. Say the question and answers out loud. Time yourself to complete the set. Can you do it faster?

Flow charts

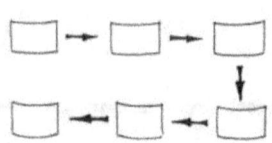

Draw flow charts for information with a sequence to give it a more visual feel.

MAKING A FLIP CHUTE

You will need:

- A clean and dry 1 litre milk carton
- Ruler
- Scissors
- Several sheets of A4 Cardboard/heavy paper
- Heavy sellotape

1. Open the top of the milk container.
2. Cut the sides of the top portion down to the top of the container.
3. Cut two slots at the front. Make slot one 4cm from the top of the container and 2.5cm deep. Make slot two 4cm from the bottom of the container and 2.5cm deep.
4. Cut one cardboard strip 16.5cm x 7cm.
5. Cut another cardboard strip 19cm x 7cm.
6. Fold down 1.2cm at both ends of the smaller strip and one end of the longer strip.
7. Insert the smaller strip and attach one end to the bottom lip of the top slot and the other end to the top lip of the bottom slot. Attach with sellotape.
8. Insert the larger strip into the container. Attach the folded end to the bottom lip of the bottom slot and then attach the top of the strip to the back of the container as shown in the picture.
9. Fold down top flaps making a box and tape into place.

10. Cut small 5cm x 6.5cm cards to write the questions on one side and answers on the other. Cut one corner off each card to make it easier to stack with questions on the same side.

> Success is adding the 'extra' to the ordinary
> —and that takes persistence.
> Bryce Courtenay

Effective Notes

MIND MAPPING TM

Mind mapping is a simple and essential skill for learning faster and retaining information. It's a creative, brain-friendly way of taking notes. It uses both the left (logical) side and the right (creative) side of the brain. This technique of note taking was developed in the early 1970s by Tony Buzan and is based on research on how your brain actually works.

Study Tip
Mind map your notes

Follow the simple steps on the following page to make your first mind map.

Step One

First, close your eyes and see the TV screen of your mind. What shape is it? Lengthways (portrait) or sideways (landscape)? Yes, it's landscape. Take a piece of blank A4 paper and turn it sideways. The paper is now imitating or copying the way your mind works inside. Even if you take your notes in the traditional way in class, it's more brain-friendly to use blank paper and turn it sideways than to take notes on ordinary lined refill.

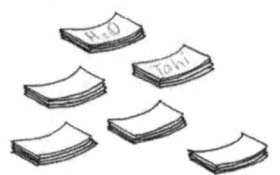

Step Two

Close your eyes again. Picture a red car on your TV screen. Where have you put it? Picture an ice cream. Where have you put it? Most people will put these images in the centre which is where your brain naturally starts. This is where you start your mind map. Using three colours, start with a picture or visual image that takes up about 5 cm in the centre of your page.

Step Three

Add the main themes like chapter headings in a book. These are printed on branches out from the central image. All the branches are always curved. All the lines on mind maps are curved because there are no straight lines in nature, so this is more 'organic' or 'brain friendly'. The theme branches are thick at the start and get thinner so the eye naturally follows the branch.

Write these key words clearly in capital letters so that they stand out. Place the words on top of lines that are the same length as the word. (See diagram below and imitate the shape.) This shape mirrors the shape of a brain cell. Write each separate branch in the same colour so that the theme and the words are all one colour. Make the lines the same colour as the words.

Step Four

Add a second level of thought like subheadings in a book. These words should link to the main branch that trigger them. Avoid using sentences. Mind maps are about using key words that will act as triggers for more information when you recall your map.

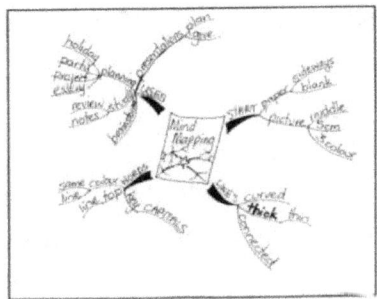

Step Five

Keep adding information. Use pictures and images where you can. Allow your thoughts to come freely so that you hop between ideas and themes.

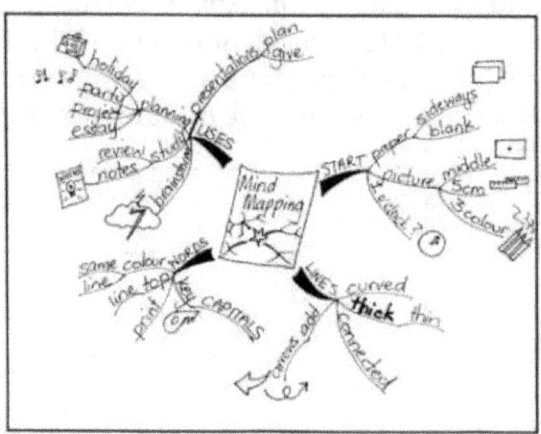

Step Six

Add dimension to your map. Highlight words, use arrows, codes and pictures. Make your mind map beautiful, colourful, artistic and imaginative. One of the good things about using mind maps is that you can add to them at any time. Unlike taking normal notes, you can fit in extra bits and pieces of information if and where you want.

Study Tip
Mind map your notes and
repeat, repeat, repeat

Taking your notes into an exam—without cheating

Using mind maps you can take your notes into the exam without cheating.

How in the world do you do this? It's as easy as a mind map! When you're studying, make mind maps for as many of your topics as possible. Practice reproducing your mind map as part of your studying. Using just one colour because it's quicker, reproduce your mind map as quickly as possible, within about two minutes. This process shouldn't be a neat and tidy process, it should be fast and messy. As long as you can read and understand the information, that is all that matters. Then check it against your original map. Using a different coloured pen, write in all the information you missed, which is the information you need to learn. Then practice reproducing the mind map again from your memory. It should only take you three or four times to be able to repeat your whole mind map from memory. Sometimes you only have to write one word and you'll remember the whole branch. When you go into the exam and the examiner says you can start, you turn over your paper and as quickly as possible reproduce your mind map. All of your notes are then in your exam and you haven't cheated. It's very, very simple.

Karen's Story

I was in Auckland recently running a seminar for teachers and met up with one of the students who had been through my workshop. He brought some of his teachers to my seminar which I thought was pretty cool. He had completed Spectrum's two day workshop about three months earlier and he said, "You know that mind mapping stuff? I mind mapped my chemistry and I got 93% in my test." His teachers couldn't believe it. All he did was mind map everything, learn the mind map and then in the exam, he wrote his mind map over the back of his exam paper. Bingo, all the information was there.

Mind mapping does take practice. Just when you learned to ride a bike, you fell off, you cried, maybe you even said I'm not going to do that for a while. Eventually you got back on. Likewise, mind mapping takes some practice, and the more you do, the easier it gets. I find I'm now thinking in mind maps, rather than lists. This is called mental mind mapping which is the next step. One good way to practice mindmaps is while you are on the phone. Turn your doodling into a mind map of what the other person is saying. Have you ever hung up the phone and when asked, "What was their news? What did they have to say?", you can't remember any of the conversation. Doing a very quick mind map while you're talking is a fast easy way to practice this skill.

NOTE MAKING

There is a difference between note taking and note making. Have you ever spent so much time writing everything a teacher says and at the end of the lesson you have no idea what you have learned? This is because you are not interacting with the information, you are merely copying information which is not very brain friendly.

Note making means you record your thoughts, ideas and questions, alongside the notes while you are listening and recording what your teacher is saying. This technique is taught by Mark Reardon, the director of Super Camp.

How to use Note Making

Take a blank page and draw a vertical line about one-third from the right hand edge. The left side of the paper is for note taking and the right side is for note making.

On the left side write your notes as the teacher talks and presents. Ensure you record the key points, terms and diagrams.

On the right record your own thoughts and feelings, reactions and questions as they come up. Write anything you think without censorship. It might say something like:

This is boring... cool idea, I'd like to learn more on this, what does that mean, who said? I'm not sure...oh that makes sense.

Writing your thoughts down in this way helps you to focus your attention and concentration on the topic and speaker. Later it will help with recall and understanding of what was written.

See my example below of a talk given by Tony Mowbray in Invercargill at a conference I attended. This is what I wrote while listening to him.

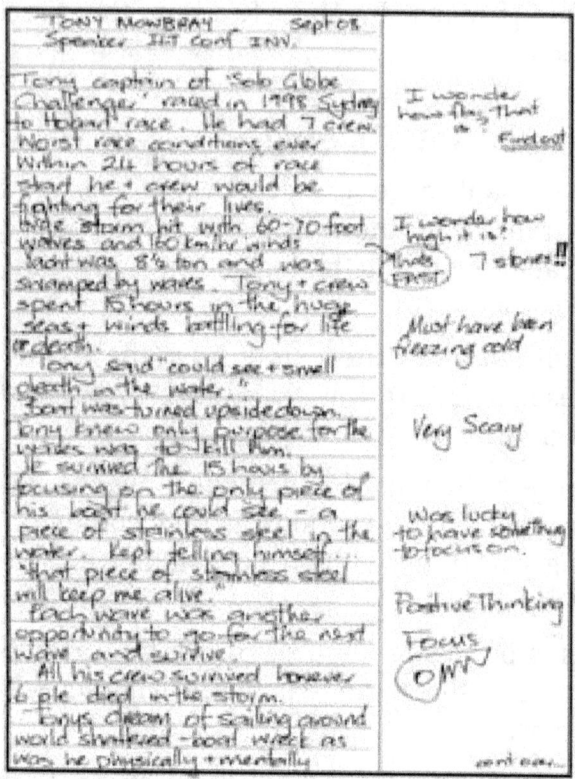

Listen and Observe Actively

Interact with the information actively by asking yourself "What are the key points?", "Is this important?", "How could I use this information in my life?", "What relevance does this have?"

Focus on what is important and going to be needed for later.

Listen for clues from your teacher: "there are 4 ways", "this might be in the exam", "the 'most' important part is..."

NOTE: If a teacher repeats information this probably means it's important. When a teacher tells a story this may be a clue to important concepts.

Participate in class

Ask questions if you are not sure. Recent research shows other students really admire people who ask questions in class because in most cases many other students had a similar question. In fact Issador Rabbi, a Nobel Prize winning Physicist, puts much of his success down to the questions that he asked rather than the information he learned. Join in with discussions. Offer your ideas and thoughts.

Visual Note Taking

Drawing pictures and diagrams is an essential part of memory. Visual note taking combines ideas from Mind MappingTM and Note Making with pictures, colour and key words. Usually what holds people back is the feeling that they can't draw. If you feel artistically challenged, you would benefit from drawing pictures in note taking. The pictures would probably be simple, funny and they would stand out!

Develop your own 'bank' of symbols. They should be easy to understand and great for your study later. Use only one side of the paper to make reviewing easier.

> ## Study Tip
> Use symbols and pictures to personalise your notes.

The pictures I draw often make me smile and I always remember them. Below is an example of my notes from the same talk by Tony Mowbray recorded with visual note taking.

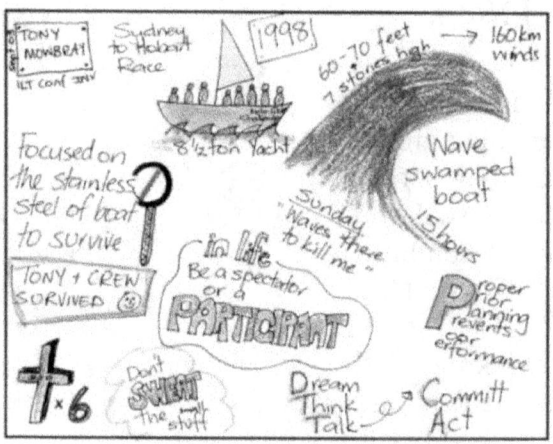

Motivation

Motivation isn't something you can have permanently. It's something you have to keep working at and a big part of this is believing in your own ability.

Creating success over and over again is as simple as following the four areas of the success cycle.

Belief

Your beliefs are a combination of your experiences and lessons since birth. They are a set of ideas about life that you hold true. Your beliefs affect your abilities. If you believe you're no good at maths, then your potential for learning in that class drops. On the other hand, if you believe you're good at maths, you're likely to keep on improving. Sometimes, the difference between being good and not so good is simply a matter of what you believe.

In life, the actions you take depend on what your

beliefs are. If you believe you will pass all your exams, you might take the extra classes offered at your school to ensure this success. When you take action, sooner or later you will get a result. Let's say you are looking for a job in the newspaper. You come to the perfect job advert. The advert is describing you, your thoughts, talents, skills and personality. You know this is your job and the starting salary is $45,000—a great starting salary for your experience level. Your beliefs about yourself and what you perceive the employer wants, will determine your action. Let's say you apply. Now you are still looking in the paper and the next week come across the same advert. Again, as you read it, your excitement mounts, as you know they are describing you. The only change to the advert now is the salary is $450,000. Would you still apply? Your beliefs may surface now. "What do they want me to do?", or "No-one is worth that much", or "I'm not intelligent enough for that job", or "That's my job!" Your beliefs will determine your actions.

Result

The results you get are feedback from your actions. You won't always get the results you want because there are always challenges in life. If your results are not what you expected, check your actions. If you are getting the results you want, then you are making useful actions.

Thought

Your thoughts are the key to achieving success. When you don't get the results you are wanting, you can have two main types of thoughts. The thought of a victim or the thought of a victor. Above or below the line of life (as described in the introduction). When things don't work out as you would like, do you become a victim by pretending your results don't matter? Or do you make excuses for why you haven't achieved your goal? Do you blame other people such as your teachers, parents or the government. "It's the Government's fault I can't find a job" is a real victim thought. Alternatively, to think like a victor is to think about taking ownership for the results and being accountable and responsible for changing your beliefs and actions to get a different result.

> **Albert Einstein said,**
> "The definition of insanity is to do the same thing and expect different results."

When successful people throughout the world get something wrong, or things don't quite work out how they expect, they take responsibility for their results and correct their beliefs and actions until they reach the desired result or outcome. And the cycle continues.

Study Tip
Say affirmations daily

Affirmations

One way to change the negative belief cycles in your mind is through affirmations. Affirmations are positive phrases that you say to yourself over and over again. This has the effect of almost reprogramming your brain. The more times you hear something (or say something to yourself) the more instant your response is to that phrase. Advertisers do this all the time. For example, if I were to begin singing "The Warehouse, The Warehouse...", I guarantee you know the tune and the next line. You probably also know the phone number for Pizza Hut whether you've ever used it or not! This is the power of programming. You can programme yourself for success with affirmations.

> What the mind can conceive and believe it will achieve.
>
> **Napolean Hill**

There are four important parts to remember about writing and saying affirmations:

1. Personalised

An affirmation must include the word "I" or "My". This is so that the focus is instantly on you. You take ownership of what you're saying. If I was to say "You're good at English", I'm talking about someone else. I need my brain to know it's me I'm talking about. So I say, "I'm good at English".

2. Positive

Affirmations must be positive. For example, if I say, "I'm not going to fail maths", which word will my brain focus on? Fail. And my brain will prove I can 'fail' maths. Make your affirmations positive. "I pass Maths easily."

3. Present Tense

Say affirmations in the present tense as if they're true already. A statement such as, "I will be good at maths..." focuses on the future. An interesting concept is that there is no future. When you get to the future where are you? In the present. There is only the present. I hear people say this: "I'll be happy when I leave school." "I'll be happy when I get a job." "I'll be happy when I get married." " I'll be happy when I have children." " I'll be happy when the children leave home." However, they forget to be happy right now. They are always putting it out in the future. But the future never comes. I was staying with a friend when her son, aged four, ran out of the bedroom and said, "Is it tomorrow yet?" Tomorrow never comes. It's always today. Say affirmations like they are true right now, for example, "I am fantastic at biology."

> Every day in every way my life
> gets better and better

4. Action

You also need to say your affirmations as if you mean them and take some sort of positive action towards the outcome. Positive thinking on it's own doesn't work. I could sit on my couch every day saying, "I'm getting fit", or go to my garden and say, "It's weed free". Of course, nothing will happen unless I take some action. If you say it like you mean it, your brain will be more likely to accept the affirmation and create the reality.

Research shows that you need to say an affirmation 20 times a day for 20 days to re-pattern your mind. Say them in the shower, walking to school, or driving in the car. Write affirmations and put them in your wallet, on your mirror, inside your folders, anywhere you will see them and remember to say them.

More Affirmations:

- I pass my exams easily and effortlessly.
- I like myself.
- I am energetic.
- I am a tidy and organised person.
- I am an excellent netball/rugby/soccer player.
- I speak clearly and precisely.
- I am great at maths.
- I am healthy and happy.
- I remember easily.
- I am calm and relaxed.
- I draw/sing well.
- My life is perfect and all my needs are met.
- I am a confident learner.

Motivation

"I am enough"

Today I am enough
I am smart enough
I am wise enough
I am clever enough
I am resourceful enough
I am able enough
I am confident enough
I am connected to enough people to accomplish
my heart's desire
I have enough ideas to pull off magic and miracles
Enough is all I need
Enough is all I have
I have more than enough

from The One Minute Millionaire by Mark Victor Hansen and Robert G Allen

There are two affirmations I suggest you say on a daily basis. The first is:

> "I pass exams easily."

If you say this 20 times a day until your exams, your brain will find a way to do it. Of course you must also take the action and study, go to class, ask questions if you are not sure, hand in assignments on time and so on.

The second affirmation is:

> "I like myself", or if you are brave enough "I love myself."

When you say this affirmation over and over again (not aloud or your friends might think you are a bit strange) your brain will automatically start focusing on all the things you like about yourself, instead of the three or four things you don't like. Have a go at saying this in the mirror looking into your own eyes. When you start to focus on the things you like about yourself, your self esteem will rise, automatically making you more successful.

> Every man is the architect of his own fortune.
> **Sallust**

Rapid Reading

It is necessary to be a good reader, as 75% of all information comes from printed material. Even the Internet is filled with pages and pages of text. Would it help to read twice as fast or three times as fast as you do now? Would it be beneficial to have better comprehension and understanding of what you read? The first step in learning to read faster is to find out what level you are reading at right now. Then, at the end of the chapter, you can test yourself and monitor your improvement.

To download the Rapid Reading Pre Test please go to http://www.spectrumeducation.com/rapid-reading/

Ask someone, or set the phone timer, to time you for one minute and start reading pre test. When the minute is up, note which line you are up to, (line numbers are down the side of the page) and multiply that number by eleven. (This is the average number of words per line.)

This is the number of words you're reading per minute right now.

No matter whether I do this pre-test with doctors, lawyers, accountants, teachers or students, the pre-test number usually averages around 250 words per minute.

Do you say the words to yourself while reading? In New Zealand, we speak at about 250 words per minute, and we read at about 250 words per minute. Our brains are actually capable of reading up to 80,000 words per minute. For full comprehension and good recall, this figure drops to about 24,000 words per minute. Just imagine how bored your brain is, if it's capable of reading 24,000 words per minute and you're only reading at around 250 words per minute.

The man who holds the world record for speed reading, Howard Berg, reads at around 24,000 words per minute, or approximately one page per second.

As nearly everyone has the ability to read quickly, one of the biggest differences between you and Howard Berg, or anyone who reads at a fast speed is your beliefs.

FOUR BELIEFS FOR RAPID READING

There are four main beliefs or ideas that need to be adopted for effective rapid reading. As you read through these, pause after each one and notice the little voice in your head. Does it say a positive comment or a negative one? Is it a belief you hold already or one you need to affirm?

Reading is easy. I read more than one word at a time. It's okay to read using my finger. I read fast and comprehend.

1. Reading is easy.

Most people, by the time they are seven years old have learned the three hardest things they will ever learn. Walking, talking and reading. There is nothing harder to learn. If you have ever watched an adult who has lost the ability to walk or talk, trying to learn again, you will know how hard it is. Learning to read as an adult is also very difficult. If you can do these three things, the great news is life can only get easier! Reading is easy!

2. I read more than one word at a time.

Well you won't be if you are saying the words to yourself as you read. This is slow and narrow or "hard focused". Rapid readers focus on the whole picture. Look outside for a moment and notice how you are more "soft focused" on the whole scene rather than on just 2cms of information. Practice seeing a page in this same way.

Action: Find a book you wish to read. Turn it upside down. Scan each page with your hand as you run your hand down the page and pick out the key words. Time yourself and take about five seconds per page or 20 pages per minute. Practice this until you can scan about 100 pages per minute, still picking out the key words from the text.

Many people are afraid they will miss words if they read fast.

Of the 600,000 words in the English language, only 400 are used 65% of the time. (Jensen, 1989) That's over half the words on a page that are "structure words" and have little or no meaning, they simply tie a sentence together.

When learning to speak, young children start with key words such as "water", "dog", "Mum". They do not say "Please can I have a drink of water". First they start with the word "water", then maybe "me water" or "water now". Structure words are the last to be learned and used.

When you are reading, skip words such as "is, to, the, and, are". Removing these words and focusing on the key words will automatically speed up your reading.

People also often think that they see every letter of each word. Count how many "f's" you see in the passage below?

Feature Films of the scientific kind are very popular especially with students of the University of Science.

There are six. Did you find them all? Or did you do what most people do and not see the 3 "of's"?

Read this one...

Paris in the the rain Did you see the two "the's"?

What about this one?

According to research at an Elingsh uinervtisy, it deosn't mttaer in waht oredr the ltteers in a wrod are, the olny iprmoatnt tihng is that the frist and lsat ltteer are in the rghit pclae. The rset can be a toatl mses and you can sitll raed it wouthit a porbelm. Tihs is bcuseae we do not raed ervey lteter by istlef but the wrod as a wlohe.

To increase your reading speed, read key words and remember the purpose of reading is to gain information, not to read every single word.

3. It's OK to read using my finger.

The last time you probably used your finger to read was at primary school. The reason teachers asked you to point to the words was so they knew that what you were reading and saying were the same thing. When you could read, you were encouraged to take your finger away to add fluency and expression. Now I'm suggesting you bring your finger back for speed. One of the reasons is because your eyes can only see something when they have stopped moving.

Action: Go into the bathroom (when no-one else is watching!) and walk up to the mirror. Smile! Now try and catch your own eyes moving. Keep your head still, just move your eyes. It is physically impossible to see your own eyes move!

When reading, it is important to keep your eyes moving quickly and smoothly.

To speed read effectively use your index finger (usually on the hand that you write with) and run it just under the text you are reading. Underline the words you are reading with your finger. The purpose of the finger is to push your eyes to work faster, therefore taking in more information.

TIP: Some people like to use a pen instead of their finger. If you find your finger is distracting then place it two or three lines below where you are reading or just in front. Remember the purpose of your finger is to keep your eyes moving or they will get lazy and slow down.

Other finger movements include sweeping the finger left- right, right-left under the text or sweeping the whole hand in a skiing motion down the page. When you increase your speed to over 1000 words per minute, you may prefer to just run your finger down the centre of the page and read either side of your finger as you go.

4. I read fast and comprehend.

Have you ever found yourself reading the same line over and over again? Have you ever found yourself reading the same line over and over again? (just kidding) Have you read to the bottom of the page and been unable to remember what you'd just read? You're reading too slowly! If your brain can cope with up to 24,000 words per minute and you are only reading at 250 words per minute, your brain is bored and your mind wanders and starts thinking about what you are going to do in the weekend, what's for tea or the conversation you had with your friend today. True isn't it? The faster you read the more your brain has to focus and comprehend. Imagine you are a world champion skier on the ski field. On the learner's slope you will be thinking about anything except your technique, staying up or how to stop. However, you are now at the top of the mountain on the hardest run of the day. As you take off you think about... skiing. Losing focus at high speed is not a good look, especially if you are attempting to impress!

FOR TECHNICAL READING:

A good sequence for reading technical material is:
Read the summary or conclusion.
Read the preface or introduction.
Preview or scan the major headings.
Examine the graphs, charts, and illustrations.
Only if you require more detail, read the main body of the text.

Comprehension is a two-fold process: perceiving and organising, and relating information to what you already know. Factors that can increase your comprehension include your background knowledge of the topic, your reading skills and the organisation and presentation of the material.

Before you read, increase your comprehension simply by scanning, looking for key words and ideas, diagram captions, headings, subheadings, bold words, italics and chapter summaries. Then read the contents and index pages. Reading the author's background and foreword can also give you insights into why they wrote the book or article which will give you a better understanding of the perspective the author is coming from.

Eliminate distractions such as TV, certain music and noisy people. Position your body so it doesn't think it's time for sleep! Sit up straight when reading, with your feet flat on the floor and your bottom forward on the seat. Ask questions about what you are reading. Having a purpose to read can increase both your comprehension and your speed.

DIFFERENT READING SPEEDS
1000-2000+

- locate specific references or words
- find an answer to a specific question
- get a general overview of a chapter, story or article

500-1000

- review something you have already read
- read magazines, comics and feature newspaper articles
- reading for pleasure—a simple novel

350-500
Fiction:

- to read difficult fiction
- to read for characterisation, theme, mood, imagery

Non-Fiction:

- find the main idea
- make generalisations
- understand patterns and sequences

250-350
Fiction:

- read complex fiction for characterisation and plot analysis

Rapid Reading

- understand relationship between characters and ideas

Non-Fiction:

- note the details, compare and contrast information
- distinguish between fact and opinion
-

100-250
Fiction:

- evaluate quality and literacy merit

Non Fiction:

- read technical or scientific material
- solve complex problems
- to follow detailed directions

Now go back and practice reading the pre-test with your finger and just picking out the key words. Remember to move your finger or hand quickly, however, not so fast that the words become a blur. You can also practice this on a book or articles you are required to read for a few minutes.

MORE TIPS ON RAPID READING

When you come to a new or unfamiliar word it is important to work out what it is. Some people think missing it out will increase your speed, however it will decrease your comprehension. Stop, look the word up in the dictionary, and maybe note down what it means for future reference. Then continue reading. Obviously there are different speeds for different kind of reading. Carolyn Coil the author of Becoming an Achiever outlines the different speeds. These are mapped out on the opposite page.

To improve comprehension, look ahead. Preview or scan everything you need to read. Quickly scan through the article or chapter before you read it. Search for key ideas and concepts. Once you have read the main headings and key phrases you will have a better idea of what it is about and your mind will be able to focus on the details.

TIRED EYES

If you have tired eyes from reading, here are three techniques for you to use. First, change your focus by looking into the distance. Focus on something far away outside your window. Next rub your hands together really fast. You will feel them getting hotter. Keep going for at least 90 seconds, until your hands are so hot you have to stop. Now cup your hands over your closed eyes, relax and breathe deeply. This should soothe your eyes. Thirdly, check your book is 35-45cm away from your eyes. This lessens eye fatigue and you can see more and therefore take more in.

TEST YOUR SPEED AGAIN

Now, test your speed again using the techniques described in this chapter. Scan through for the key words. Use your finger to keep your eyes moving, and read to understand not memorise.

Download the Rapid Reading Post Test from http://www.spectrumeducation.com/rapid-reading/

Read for one minute and again notice the line number you finish at.

This article is a little more technical than the first. Multiply your line number by 9 (the average number of words per line). What's your speed now? How much have you improved? Now check your comprehension.

RAPID READING COURSES

I've taught many rapid reading courses and when I meet a student who's completed one of my rapid reading workshops, I often ask them, "How is your rapid reading going?" They usually reply, "Oh, it didn't work!" In fact, what they really mean is... they stopped practicing. You've got to keep practicing to keep your speed up.

If you wanted to be an Olympic swimmer and you turned up to the first day of training, swim 3 kilometres, and then didn't bother to turn up for training for the rest of the year, would you get to go to the Olympic Games? No. Because you have to put the training in first, whether it's swimming, running or reading. Many people tell me the rapid reading didn't work but what they really mean is that they didn't practise and didn't continue. Practising is very simple. Every time you pick up a book, a magazine or a newspaper, it's an opportunity to practise your rapid reading. It's more effective to practise on easy material, because if you practise on books with big technical words, your brain will take a little bit longer to read those words. Treat rapid reading like organised sport. Practise on easy material and practise often to increase your reading speed. If you want to increase it quickly, keep practising every day.

> **Henry Ford said**
> "If you think you can or think you can't -
> you're absolutely right"

Success And Mistakes

There are several factors that successful people use to ensure continued success. One is their posture or physiology. Successful people also understand to be successful they will make mistakes. In this chapter you'll read about both these factors.

Physiology(BodyLanguage)

What you do with your body, or physiology, makes a huge difference to your ability to learn and be successful. If I told you that were about to meet a highly depressed person, what kind of person would you imagine? If I said you were about to meet a highly successful, motivated person, who would you imagine? The first person might have their head and shoulders down, be dragging their feet and sighing, and the second person might have an upright posture, make lots of eye contact and be breathing deeply. Your physiology can determine how you actually feel. Communication is more than just words. In fact, it is made up of three key components. Your words, tonality and physiology.

Often, it's not what you say, but how you say it. If a person is slouched in their chair and, talking in a slow monotone voice, says, "I'm really excited about my new assignment", the listener picks up the real message from the tonality and physiology, rather than from the words.

When you are in a positive physiology, such as sitting up smiling, chemicals called endorphins are released in the brain. (Endorphins make you feel good).

Exercise and chocolate sends the same chemicals through your brain making you feel great. When you are in poor physiology, slouching or depressed, your body releases cortisol which is a stress hormone, making you feel worse. Cortisol is linked to many major illnesses.

There are times when you will sit down to study and it is the last place you want to be. In fact, throughout your life you will be required to do many things you don't wish to do. If you sit there and sigh, slouch and feel bad, it will be hard to concentrate and difficult to comprehend your information. It will take a long time to learn your information. However if you "act as if" you want to study by sitting up and smiling, you'll feel better and it will be easier to concentrate and comprehend. You'll get your study completed in record time, and you'll still be able to go out and do what you really want.

There are many fantastic examples from history that show how mistakes and failures can lead to success.

Study Tip
Check your physiology before sitting down to study

Mistakes

Making mistakes is a great way to learn. Think about how a baby learns to walk They pull themselves up, take that fantastic first step and... fall down. They pull themselves back up again and fall again. This learning process applies to other tasks such as reading, writing, maths, learning to ride a bike, roller skate or drive a car.

High achievers are made not born. They make mistakes and learn from them. Babe Ruth, world famous baseball player, held the world record for the number of home runs hit in his lifetime—714. He also held the world record for the number of strike outs—1330. He struck out nearly twice as many times as he hit home runs, and was the most successful at both.

When making a movie, a director will shoot as many "takes" as necessary to get the best shot. Each time the scene is not correct the director calls it a mis-take and asks the crew to do it again, with the necessary corrections. This is a major key to learning from mistakes. Recognise where you went wrong and correct it. A six-year-old once explained this to me as a maze. "When you come to a dead end, you go back and find out where you went wrong and take another path."

Did you know...

- Michael Jordan failed to make his secondary school's basketball team.
- Walt Disney was fired from a newspaper, because he lacked "good creative ideas".
- Einstein could not speak until be was four and did not learn to read until he was seven.
- Beethoven's music teacher told him he was "hopeless as a composer".

Study Tip
Learn from your mistakes

Fear of Failure

Many people are scared of failing and do not attempt new tasks and activities for fear of not getting it right. This is crazy. You learn from making mistakes. Often people use excuses to stop them experiencing failure. Have you ever heard yourself (or people around you) saying something like this?

"Why should I study, I'm going to fail anyway."

"That teacher doesn't like me. He'll fail me no matter what I do."

"Why should I do anything my Mum wants? She thinks everything I do is wrong no matter what."

This negative self-talk is not success talk. People who talk like this often sound tough and act as though they have everything under control. On the inside, their self confidence is usually really low.

In Mark Victor Hansen's Book The One Minute Millionaire, he discusses a SNAP technique for eliminating negative self-talk. Simply put a rubber band around your wrist. Every time you catch yourself having a negative thought, simply snap the rubber band. Ouch! He suggests you wear the band for 30 days, 24 hours a day. Give it a go. It works!

The American poppy grower goes out to his poppy fields one day and sees a single poppy standing one metre tall among all the other 30cm poppies. The farmer is excited and rushes over to the poppy and thinks, "How can I get all my poppies to grow this tall?"

The New Zealand poppy farmer goes out to his poppy fields one day and sees a single poppy standing one metre tall among all the other 30cm poppies. The farmer rushes over to the poppy and, taking a pair of scissors from his pocket, cuts it down.

FEAR stands for False Expectations Appearing Real. It is when you think forward to a situation in your mind and see a negative outcome and bring this image back to the present and then worry or get fearful about what might happen. It is a false expectation that you created in your head and then have made it seem real.

Anthony Robbins says, "The past does not equal the future." Just because you failed last year, yesterday, or two minutes ago does not mean you will fail today, tomorrow or on your next attempt.

Fear Of Success

Sometimes people fear being successful. What will people think? What if my friends don't like or accept me anymore. It's called the Tall Poppy Syndrome and it's very common in New Zealand and Australia. In general, Americans do not have this syndrome. Here is an example of the Tall Poppy Syndrome.

> Most people fail in life because they major in minor things.
> **Anthony Robbins**

Goal Setting

In Alice in Wonderland, one scene has Alice completely and thoroughly lost, not knowing which way to turn. She asks the Cheshire Cat, perched on a tree limb, for some help.

"Would you tell me, please, which way I ought to go from here?" asks Alice.

"That depends a good deal on where you want to go," replies the cat.

"I don't much care where," says Alice.

"Then it doesn't much matter which way you go," came the reply.

Goals are critical to your success. In life, it is essential you know in which direction you are heading or you'll end up some place you don't want to be.

There are five keys to successful goal setting.

SMART goals
Specific

Your goals must be very specific. If I set a goal that states, "I want to be successful" it doesn't say at what.

You get what you ask for in life. How can you get what you want out of life if you don't tell anyone, or you don't know what you want?

Make sure the goals you set are specific.

Karen's Story

A young girl was working in the Spectrum office several years ago. It was her birthday and I wanted to buy her a birthday gift and was unsure of what to buy her or indeed what was appropriate. So I asked her. "What would you like for your birthday?" She answered "I dunno." Well, I don't know what dunno is so I didn't buy her anything. She learned on that day to be specific. If people ask you what you want, tell them. Now you may not always get what you want, but if you don't ask you definitely won't get it. Children are great at this. They ask and ask and ask, and often wear down their parents until they say yes.

Goal Setting

Measurable

Your goals must also be measurable. What would happen if you ran a marathon and there was no finish line? How would you know when you had completed the run? You would either stop short or keep going well past the finish line.

Make your goals measurable so that you will know when you have achieved a goal and celebrate your success.

Achievable

Set your goals so they are achievable. If you want to be an Olympic swimmer and you don't know how to swim, this goal may be too big. If you want to be an interpreter and you are good at maths and not at languages, you may want to reconsider.

A friend once set a goal to run a particular half marathon in 2 hours and 22 minutes. She wrote her goal down and displayed it so she could see it daily.

This goal was an achievable goal for her, but not for me because I don't run!

Future NZ Olympian Story

I met a 17 year old girl in Auckland recently. She told me her goal is to be in the next Olympic team, representing NZ in the long jump. She explained she has a tape measure above her bedroom door with red marks on it at exactly the distances she needs to jump to achieve her goal. That's making a goal really measurable.

When she ran the half marathon the stop watch stopped at 2 hours and 22 minutes!

Realistic

I asked my friend, "What if you had set that goal for 2 hours and 18 minutes?" She replied that at the time this was not realistic, however it is now. The difference between achievable and realistic is that it is achievable for everyone reading this book to pass every exam you sit. What will be different is, realistically, are you willing to do what it takes? Are you willing to study, ask questions if you are not sure, learn the information you got wrong, practice old exam papers, use colour and effective note taking and so on.

Are you willing to do what it takes to achieve your goals?

Time Frame

It's also important to put a date or time frame on your goals. When do you want to achieve this goal? A time frame creates urgency. If I say my goal is to get my homework complete it doesn't say when. If I say, "My goal is to complete my homework by next weekend" there is a bit more urgency to get on with it.

Successful Goal Setting

> **Karen's Story**
>
> One of my long term goals is to learn how to fly a plane. When I travelled in smaller planes, before the aviation security rules tightened, I asked to sit in the "jump seat" behind the pilot in the cockpit. Nearly always they say yes. I learned how to read the displays and the procedures for flying for free! When telling people I flew in the cockpit I usually got the same response. How did you get to do that? My reply, I asked.

Write your goals down. What marks do you want in each subject? Check each time you sit a test or get an assignment back. Are your marks on track for you to achieve your goal? Do you need to change your approach to reach your goal?

Dreams don't come true magically. They usually become a reality slowly through experiences and encouragement from others.

Once you know what your goal is, you must plan the steps involved to complete it. If your goal is to get your driver's licence and you have done nothing towards achieving this goal, the first step would be to get a road code. Next would be to learn it. (Notice I didn't just say read it. Just because you read something does not mean you have learned it.) Step three would be to sit and pass your written test. Now you can find a teacher to teach you to drive. Then you can practice for six months and book the test, sit and pass and you have your licence. Now of course you may slip up on a step and all the steps are not the same height. If you do, learn from your mistakes and do it again.

If you are not sure of the steps involved, you could use the Planning Evaluation Review Technique (PERT) that NASA used to put a man on the moon. You start with the final outcome and work backwards and ask, "What happened just before that?"

> **Study Tip**
> Set goals and achieve them
> step by step

> You don't start climbing a mountain to get to the middle. Why be content with being in the middle?
>
> **James Hart**

A way to fast-track your goals is to model successful people and find mentors. Successful people love helping others become successful. Just ask.

Find people who have already succeeded at something you want to do. Find role models who have overcome obstacles. Read books about successful people. Watch documentaries about people who have achieved. Take a successful person out for lunch.

Remember that some successful people have also done things that are not useful. Some successful music stars also use drugs. This has not helped them be successful. Make sure you model the good things only.

Study Tip
Model successful people

Success Story

Olympic pentathlete, Marilyn King, is a great example of how well visualisation works.

She had trained hard for three years, and there was one more year before the Olympics. Just as she was gearing up to peak before the Olympics, she had a serious car accident. She was laid upon her back in hospital for six months.

Without any opportunity for physical training, Marilyn practised her routines over and over in her mind. Every day, she exercised with visualisations.

When she finally left hospital, she had just two months to get fit for the pentathlon, one of the most gruelling events at the Olympics.

At her first physical try-out her coach was amazed. Her muscles and fitness were at such a level that she was able to bring her fitness up to Olympic level in just four weeks from leaving hospital. Her mind had literally trained and toned her body.

She not only succeeded in passing the trials, she succeeded at the Olympic Games.

Visualisation

Visualise your success daily. The power of such a simple tool as visualisation is immense. Napoleon Hill, author of Think and Grow Rich said, "What the mind can conceive and believe it will achieve."

Have you seen yourself being successful? Have you seen yourself passing your exams?

The mental images you create are important.

Believe you can succeed and expect success.

Study Tip
Visualise your success daily

Time Management

Managing your time is an important part of being successful with passing exams and life.

All successful, healthy, happy, wealthy and famous people have one thing in common. They all have the same amount of hours each day. What they do differently is how they use those hours.

Imagine your bank gives you $86,400 per day, every day, and you can not carry any money over to the next day. At midnight each day your bank deletes anything that is left in your account. What would you do with it? How would you spend it? You would draw out every cent every day.

We all have the same time bank. 86,400 seconds each day and you can not take any over to the next day or get any more. Once you have used or not used your time there is no going back. Invest those seconds wisely.

Planning your day and study time makes a remarkable difference to how much you can achieve.

Success Story

When Charles M. Schwab was President of a huge American Steel works, he asked I.V. Lee, a management consultant, for a way to get more things done. He added an unusual challenge. He said "If it works, I'll pay you anything within reason." Lee passed Schwab a piece of paper and said, "Write down all the tasks you have to complete tomorrow." Then he asked him to "number the items in order of real importance". After Schwab had done that, Lee concluded by telling Schwab to start with number one and keep doing it until it was complete. Then he told him to move to number two, but don't go any further until that task is complete. Next complete task three. He said if you can't get everything on the list done in one day at least you will have completed the most important things. Lee advised Schwab to do this every day and when you are convinced, get your team to test it, then send me a cheque for what you think the idea is worth. In a few weeks Schwab sent Lee a cheque for $25,000. Schwab later stated it was the most profitable idea he had ever learned in his business career.

Way back in 1895 Vilfredo Pareto, an Italian sociologist, founded the 80:20 rule. He said that 80% of the value was in 20% of the time spent. This Pareto principle does not only apply to time management.

- 80% of the time you eat out will be at 20% of the restaurants.
- 20% of your clothes get 80% of the wear.

- 80% of the interruptions you get come from 20% of the people.
- In sales, 80% of the sales will come from 20% of your customers.

People often focus on the low priority tasks rather than on the important tasks that get the real results.

Writing a list of all the tasks you need to complete is a start.

Then you Prioritise the list.

Keep your list of tasks manageable by having no more than seven tasks. If you complete these in a day write another list.

There is also a difference between urgent and important tasks. It would be urgent to complete an assignment due tomorrow and important to start planning an essay due in three weeks. Urgent tasks take more energy and focus and are often not your best work, because it is often rushed. Concentrate on important tasks before they become urgent

Ask yourself the question, "Is this the best use of my time right now?" If the answer is no, work out what is?

Avoid time wasters. There are literally thousands of time wasters around us. They stop you doing the really important things.

Prioritise your list as follows:

- urgent
- important
- some value
- don't do

and do the A's first!

You may identify with some of the following time wasters:

- going off on tangents all the time
- procrastination—putting things off
- over planning
- under planning
- doing too many things at once
- not sticking to deadlines
- stopping other people from working
- not using your diary effectively
- having a cluttered desk
- trying to please everyone
- watching too much TV
- looking at effort rather than results
- computers/videos/Internet
- ringing/texting a friend instead of working
- futzing*
- Futzing describes what people are doing when they are wasting time on computers. This is spending 70 minutes deciding on the font you want to use or spending 45 minutes choosing the background colours for your screen and another 20 minutes finding a screen saver. If it's not important then it is a waste of time.

Proper

Prior

Planning

Prevents

Poor

Performance

Create More Time

I often hear students say there is not enough time in the day to study and then find out they spend several hours a day on the internet, playing games or watching TV. To create more time think about this... If you watched one hour less TV or computer time per day, that's seven hours a week you have to achieve your goals. This translates to 30 extra hours a month and 360 extra hours a year or 15 whole days. Limit yourself to TV that is going to help inspire you to achieve your goals. If you are going to watch TV, watch documentaries about people who have achieved great things or overcome major challenges in their life.

What could you achieve with 15 extra days per year?

What if you reduced your TV and computer time by 2 hours a day. That's an extra month a year. The possibilities are endless.

While writing this section of the book, I asked Robyn Pearce, Australasia's time management expert for some tips to share with you. Here is what she suggested:

Chunk out your study time, and work to a plan.

When you look at the whole project it often feels too big, too overwhelming. Instead, break it into small pieces and you can easily get a grip on just how much work you need to invest each day. Ask yourself: "When is the assignment or exam due? How many weeks have I got?" Work backwards from the final date, cutting some slack for days off, or times when you're too busy to work. Also leave a realistic chunk of time for review or editing (if it's an assignment) at the end. If you start early enough, you'll be delighted how surprisingly little time is needed per day. In one quick stroke your thinking changes from, "This is too much" to "I can do this!"

Use prompts to keep you on track

Rule up a chart showing as many little squares as chunks to your goal, and record the goal date for completion. Each day tick off the number of chunks you've done. Something so simple is amazingly motivating, especially if you like to "see" progress.

Another idea is to ring a bell each time you reach a milestone.

You may prefer to have a dish on your desk or in your room with as many marbles or pretty pebbles as there are components in your task. Each day, as you complete your allocation, transfer the corresponding number of marbles into another dish.

Do the big job first

Many people try and get the little things handled before they start on their big tasks. The outcome?

The important tasks pile up, and they get bogged down in minutiae and perfectionism. Instead, handle the things that really matter first. You'll be amazed at how the small activities fit in and around the important activities. Do the study first, and then you've got the rest of the day (or evening if you like to study after school or work) to do everything else.

> It is not enough to be busy.
> The question is what are we busy about.
> Henry David Thoreau

Learn to say 'no'

If you can politely say "no" when asked to invest time into activities that don't match your goals, you consistently achieve more. Listen to your intuition—it will guide you.

Do it better

Always look for ways to shorten and improve your process. Hold a permanent question in your mind: "How can I improve?" The danger is that we fall into a comfort zone, and don't want to change. Welcome the opportunity to improve.

Eliminate clutter

Messy desk, house, bedroom, office, garage, car—it doesn't matter what it is. When things are lying around, your subconscious mind has to work harder to ignore the 'mind traffic' distractions; you become slower and less effective.

Do yourself a favour—clear up your work space before you start (but don't let that be a procrastination device!), and then keep it going—put away as you go. The feeling of freedom is its own reward.

About Robyn:

Robyn is Managing Director of TimeLogic. She has written many books including: *Getting A Grip On Time, About Time—120 Tips for Those with No Time* and *Getting A Grip On The Paper War*. These are available at www.gettingagripontime.com

---

> Make a decision to study and do it.

Use your school diary

Write in all assignments due and test dates. Plan when you are going to study and write it down. I have even ripped pages out of my diary so no-one can book me on that day and I can work on my goals.

Colour-code days off and study days to give you a quick check as to what kind of day it is.

Eliminating Procrastination

Step 1

Write a daily action list.

Step 2

Cut the overwhelming 'A' tasks into chunks.

Step 3

Do the 'A' tasks first.

Step 4

Turn difficult tasks into a game by giving yourself a challenge to finish something in a certain time or make less mistakes than last time. Keep score to make it fun.

Step 5

Commit to a deadline. I am meeting a colleague at the airport tonight at 9.30pm and I have instructed him to ask me if I have finished this book? So I have a deadline and someone who is going to check up on me!

Step 6

Create a reward system. Each time you complete a major chunk, reward yourself. It may be a five-minute walk out in the sun, lunch or a quick phone call to a friend.

Exam Techniques

The first thing I recommend you do when you are allowed to start, is to quickly read through the entire exam paper. Scan it quickly, looking at the questions to see what will be required to pass this exam.

Once you have an overview of what you are dealing with, start with the easy questions first. This will help calm you and build your confidence.

Allow your subconscious to work on the harder questions while you are doing the easier ones.

By the time you get to the harder questions your subconscious mind will have come up with some ideas and answers. Plus some of the easy questions and answers may have triggered information for the harder questions.

> **Study Tip**
> Quickly read through the entire exam paper, go back, do the easy questions first, then the hard ones

When writing your answers, make it easy for the examiner to understand your thought process. Examiners look for concise, readable, well-presented work that answers the question. Short sentences are best. Use simple words. Using long words inappropriately or words that you don't fully understand will not impress the marker. It will give the impression you are trying to bluff your way through. Marks will be lost accordingly. Go for simplicity of wording and shorter sentences. Make sure your handwriting is easy to read.

Here is a list of words you may find in an exam paper and what they mean:

- Analyse

Take to pieces what occurred and determine what makes up the various parts. This involves examining something minutely and critically.

- Compare

Liken one thing with another. What are the similarities or differences.

- Contrast

What are the differences between them, including the degree of difference if any.

- Define

Give the exact meaning and describe the essential qualities.

- Describe

    Explain the features, qualities or properties in detail.

- Discuss

    Debate the positives and negatives.

- Evaluate

    Explain the meaning and analyse (take apart the whole) then put the important points together and comment or make judgement on it.

- Explain

    Make plain and clear and give the meaning of.

- Illustrate

    Make clear and explain with a description, examples and diagrams.

- Justify

    Prove or show to be just or right.

- List

    Number the items down the page.

- Outline

    Give the main features and ideas, facts or principals.

- State

    Formally set out the facts clearly.

- Summarise

    Give a clear account of the main points.

Before the exam

- Get a great night's sleep, and remember cramming isn't a smart option.
- Eat a healthy breakfast and/or lunch if it is an afternoon exam.
- Relax and quietly review the key points an hour before your exam.
- Ensure you have all your pens, rulers, calculator and spare batteries etc.
- Get to your exam 15-20 minutes early.
- Keep yourself positive by telling yourself to relax and visualising a successful exam.
- Avoid people who are stressing out and speaking negatively about the exam.

In the Exam

- Once you find your seat get organised by spreading out your pens, pencils etc.
- Read the instructions carefully.
- Divide your time according to the marks. If it's a three hour exam and there are three sections, each section should take 50-55mins, allowing time for reviewing at the end. If there are 40 multi-choice questions in a section you have just over one minute per question.
- Ensure you answer the compulsory questions.
- Remember to answer every question.
- If you are running out of time, make sure you get down the main points.

- Space out answers so it is easy for the marker to read. A good rule is to start each new question on a new page. Label each question clearly. Number the pages to avoid any confusion.
- If you make a mistake, clearly cross it out and start again.
- At the end, if you have time, proof read your answers, check mathematical answers and working.
- For numerical questions you should show your working steps. Marks are often allocated for each step so that if you make an error along the way, you may still be able to get good marks
- For questions requiring descriptive answers, use the mark allocation as a guide to the number of points required. For example, to answer a 2-mark question fully, you are likely to be required to give two distinctly different points.
- Include, where possible, an equation or sketch wherever relevant.

What to do when you can't think of an answer

Take a deep breath, stretch and look up to recall the information. If you can't recall a date, leave a space and come back to it later. If you are not sure about the answer, jot down a couple of points on the exam paper and tell yourself you will come back to the question after you have completed the next two. If you have forgotten some of your material, ask yourself these questions:

- Where was I when studying this?

- What was I thinking?
- What did I say?
- What letter of the alphabet did it start with?

Exam Stress

If you are feeling stressed before an exam, it is likely that you are seeing a negative or bad result inside your head. Make sure you are using positive self talk, affirmations, and are seeing a positive result. Visualise yourself going into the exam calm and relaxed. See yourself scanning through the paper and starting with the easy questions first. Feel yourself calmly writing the answers and the information flowing out of the end of your pen. See yourself successfully completing the paper with time to spare for a check of all questions. Imagine yourself walking out of the exam feeling confident and knowing you have completed the paper to the best of your ability.

12

Final Thoughts

If you have completed the work throughout the year and have used the tips in this book, and know your information, you will do well in your exams. Remember the effort you have put in during your study will reflect in your exam results.

Study Smart and Pass

Finally, I Wish You Enough

I wish you enough rain to make you appreciate the sun I wish you enough happiness to keep your spirit alive

I wish you enough sadness so that you appreciate the smallest joys in life

I wish you enough gain to satisfy your ambitions

I wish you enough loss to appreciate all that you possess

I wish you enough love so you know just how special you are

I wish you enough hurt to make love even sweeter

I wish you enough dreams to cause your imagination to soar

I wish you enough reality to keep your feet on the ground

I wish you enough success to make you proud

I wish you enough failure to keep you humble

I wish you enough independence to accomplish your goals

I wish you enough dependence on others to keep your goals from being selfish

I wish you enough "hellos" to get you through the final "good-bye" Source unknown

Study Tips Summary

- Learn the information I don't know
- Everything is hard before it is easy
- Use lots of colour
- Talk about your information
- Move around while you're learning
- Frame important information
- When studying, eat brain food at least once an hour
- Drink at least 6-8 glasses of water a day
- Study with low lighting
- Study to music without words
- Play Baroque music quietly in the background while studying
- Wear comfortable clothes during exams
- Practise old exam papers
- Practise writing before an exam
- Study at your best thinking time
- Get everything ready before you begin studying
- Do exam aerobics
- Put all information up high
- When you can't remember something, look up
- Learn your most important information first
- Revise your most important information last
- Study for 20 minutes and take a 5 minute break
- Go over your notes one day after learning them,

then one week later, one month later, then every six months
- Make up stories and mnemonics about your information
- Learn only three or four things at a time
- Create real life examples
- Draw pictures and diagrams
- Mind map your notes
- Mind map your notes and repeat, repeat, repeat
- Use symbols and pictures to personalise your notes
- Say affirmations daily
- Practise rapid reading at least once a week
- Check your physiology before sitting down to study
- Learn from your mistakes
- Set goals and achieve them step by step
- Model successful people
- Visualise your success daily

Bibliography

Batmanghelidj, F. MD. Your Body's Many Cries For Water. Global Health Solutions Inc, USA, 1997.

Boyes, Karen. 27 Study Tips for Success. Spectrum Education, NZ, 2000

Boyes, Karen. Creating An Effective Learning Environment. Spectrum Education, NZ, 2001.

Buzan, Tony. The Mind Map Book. BBC Books, UK, 1993.

Canfield, Jack and Mark Victor Hansen. Chicken Soup for the Soul. Health Communications Inc, Florida, USA, 1993.

Canfield, Jack, Mark Victor Hansen and Les Hewitt. The Power Of Focus. Vermilion, London, 2000.

Coil, Carolyn. Becoming An Achiever—a student guide. Hawker Brownlow Education, Australia, 1994.

Coster, Niall. Success With Study. Coster Publications, Christchurch, NZ, 1987.

Deporter, Bobbi. Quantum Learning. Dell Publishing, New York, USA, 1992.

Dryden, Gordon and Dr Jeannette Vos. The Learning Revolution. The Learning Web Ltd, NZ, 1997.

Jensen, Eric. Student Success Secrets. Barron's Educational Series Inc, USA, 1989.

Kedgley, Sue. Eating Safely in a Toxic World. Penguin Books, NZ, 1998.

Kroehert, Gary. Taming Time or How Do You Eat An Elephant. McGraw-Hill, Australia, 1999.

Morrison, Kim and Fleur Whelligan. Like Chocolate for Women. Tandem Press, Auckland, NZ, 2001.

North, Vanda with Tony Buzan. Get Ahead. Mind Map Your Way To Success. Oakdale Printing Co Ltd, Dorset, 1991.

Pearce, Robyn. Getting A Grip On Time. Reed, NZ, 1996.

Robbins, Anthony. Unlimited Power. Simon & Schuster Ltd, London, 1986.

Rose, Colin. Accelerated Learning. Dell Publishing, USA, 1985.

Rose, Colin. Master It Faster. Accelerated Learning Systems Ltd, UK, 1999.

Sousa, David A. How The Brain Learns. Corwin Press Inc, California, USA, 2001.

Victor Hansen, Mark and Robert G. Allen. One Minute Millionaire. Random House, Australia, 2002.

Acknowledgements

This book is the result of working with thousands of teachers and students throughout the world, who have shared their success stories from their classrooms and personal study and have taken my ideas and tested them out ... Thanks.

To all those people who have contributed personally to this book especially Kim Morrison, Robyn Pearce and Zoe Eggleton, my sincere thanks

Thanks to Dixie Carlton, my book coach, for graciously sharing your expertise and believing in me to play a bigger game.

Thanks to Mark McKeon and Angie Belcher who have generously given me permission to print extracts of their work in order to support your efforts to study effectively.

To the current and past team at Spectrum, thanks for all the help, advice, feedback and new learning and insights. You are an awesome group of people, focused on our goal of being At the Heart of Teaching & Learning.

And to the silent and most supportive team members I have—my family. Tui and Trevor who have quietly supported from the side lines with incredible faith and love.

Finally, to my biggest fans, Hamish and Sasha for being great teenagers and a constant inspiration and joy. You give me the drive to ensure yours and others education will be a positive and worthwhile experience. And Denny, whose love and support is immense and valued more than you will ever understand. Thanks for being the best Dad to our children and the most incredible husband in the world. I love you with all my heart and soul.

www.ingramcontent.com/pod-product-compliance
Lightning Source LLC
Chambersburg PA
CBHW050556300426
44112CB00013B/1945